*Tales of the Route*

Proudly Printed In The United States of America

**$19.97 US / $27.97 CAN**

**Pest Control**

**Outer Marker Publishing**
Ocala, FL
OuterMarkerPublishing.com

**ISBN-13:**
**978-1475041491**

**ISBN-10:**
**1475041497**

Jerry Schappert

*I dedicate this work to my best friend who has stuck by my side during all the ups and downs of my career. Whose belief in me has stirred up the confidence and conviction I needed to reach almost every meaningful goal in my life. To the one person who was not afraid to share my dreams; not only in ideas but also in the action and physical toil it took achieve them. To this friend I say Thank You for completing this once 1/2 person and walking with me on this long and sometimes lonely road. If in this life I am even minutely successful, I owe thanks to only two. To God Almighty whose grace I cannot comprehend and to my best friend while here on this earth, my loving and adoring wife.*

# The Hollow Mansion on 39th

Pulling into the brick driveway so beautifully outlined with mature green hedges with flowers at their feet, it's hard to imagine that just seconds ago I was on one of the busiest streets in Baltimore. I'm sure the builder didn't envision this stately structure would have much more traffic than the occasional chauffeur driven Rolls Royce or even a fine horse drawn carriage. Fast forward 60 or more years and the passing roar of cars and trucks was now continual. While many cities and towns have defined lines where neighborhoods change and homes take on the look of their surroundings, this street was caught in the middle of what used to be and what couldn't be stopped from coming. These homes are still so beautiful with old growth trees, grand architecture, and hidden gardens tucked away on their half acre plots while just a mere two blocks away is a 24 hour 'cash and dash' and one of the busiest places of the city.

Such was one street on my first pest control route. I serviced several of these old glorious homes and always came away with a sense of sadness each time they came up for service. The people were for the most part the original families and no doubt helplessly watched as their beautiful homes were swallowed up in progress. This is the story of one of those customers who lived on this street and although the story is somewhat unique, it was much the same for all of my clients who lived on this once elegant and prestigious thoroughfare. With only memories of days gone by when they were once the envy of the surrounding world, they quietly watched the busy world swallow them up from the lonely but beautiful windows in their hollow mansions on 39th.

## First Impressions

I don't remember what the original service call was for, but there I was standing in the foyer of a large and impressive home. Greeted by a majestic staircase that wrapped around the entrance with a huge chandelier suspended from a very high ceiling. The wood work of the hand rails and balusters was obviously handmade with actual scenes and faces painstakingly carved into every corner or knob. The deep dark brown color of the high paneled walls spoke of royalty and privilege. A grand piano sat quietly in the huge family room and built in shelves packed with books and small collectibles from around the world filled the awe-inspiring room. The detail in craftsmanship was everywhere, even the old steam heat registers looked as if they were hand crafted from solid gold. There didn't seem to be a lot of furniture, but what was there was top of the line and looked very expensive. I was summoned to the summer porch where I was met by the owner of the house.

The bright and cheery lanai was no less beautiful and was, by the looks of things, the place where this lady spent most of her time. The windows vaulted up to the ceiling and the view of a beautiful rose garden and small pond made you forget you were in the middle of the city. She introduced herself as Dr. Muriez and I was a bit taken aback. She was a small, gray-haired, unassuming lady with glasses perched on the end of her nose. She spoke broken english and at first look you might guess her to be the housekeeper, not some doctor, and certainly not the owner of such a magnificent estate, or world traveler. She cleared a pile of newspapers and cut coupons off of a patio chair and we sat down to discuss my treatment plan. I believe she wanted to check me out because she was leery of pesticides but I found her questions were well thought out and reasonable. I think I must have satisfied her because soon we were off and running with her treatment. She led the way.

## The Grand Tour

The first floor was indeed a thing to behold. Each room was more gorgeous than the next and fit for any king. The good doctor accompanied me throughout, holding the door as if she were a tour guide and telling me the many stories behind the many paintings and decor. Statues from Africa, artifacts from Egypt, books from around the world- the home was definitely filled with a history and at least at one time this home was filled with life. Nothing was overdone mind you, but it was obvious she had been the only occupant for quite a long time. Although grand, there was the inescapable feeling of emptiness that no amount of past glory could erase.

Our conversation flowed somewhat as her broken vocabulary allowed. I remember her keen interest in my service. She was thankful of how attentive and careful I was. She was amazed that she had to sign a one year contract for what she thought was a simple problem. But if she had to have 12 treatments, it was obvious she was going to make the most of them and she watched to make sure I obliged. I don't recall even seeing a bug, but being a rookie, I wasn't aware there was anything but monthly service. It seemed like time flew because she was so interesting. I felt she was happy with me as well. The mood noticeably changed however, as we made our way around the silent piano into the foyer and came face to face with the impressive staircase. The highly polished finish gleamed in the foyers dim light, but it was clear these stairs had not been used in a very long time, at least not in any joyful or meaningful way.

Coming to the stairs, the doctor paused for a moment as if to gain her composure. She complimented me on my service and said she was surprised I was so new on the job. We slowly made our way up the elegant staircase which led up to a very long hallway with many doors on either side. Dr. Muriez opened each one, but this time there wasn't any announcement of the rooms use or stories of days gone by. The rooms were darkened except for a few beams of sunlight that pierced through the old and worn curtains.

For the most part, the once lived in spaces were empty. The belongings that had been left inside, were for years  untouched and covered in white sheets that were gray from dust. I felt like I was in some sort of mausoleum and the first to visit any of these rooms in decades. There were no pictures on the walls, no trinkets from exotic world travels, and no stories from the doctor.  I was so curious to ask about its obvious demise but knew this was one subject I should not approach. Yet for all that was missing, the walls spoke volumes. What they described was a sad, lonely, and perhaps a tragic past. Just as it was unthinkable that this magnificent home could be nestled inside such a chaotic part of the city, it was even more unimaginable that the second and third floors were so dark and lifeless above the grand living area below.

## 12 Treatments Couldn't Break The Barrier

As with any mega pest control company, the service contract was monthly, for a year whether you needed it or not. With each visit, I came to know Dr. Muriez a little better, but there was always a line I could not cross. She looked forward to my coming and was always ready with another story of her experiences around the world. There was always some sadness, a lonely empty void that in her broken english she couldn't explain or I couldn't understand. She never talked of family much. Love was something, I imagine, had escaped her all her life, or maybe she had just shut out. It was never more obvious then when we walked up the stairs to treat the upper floors of her large and impressive home. With each step upwards, her fond recollections and vivid memories grew colder and quieter. By the time we'd reach the hall and its many doors, the only sound was that of our hollow footsteps on the once polished and well-traveled floors.

With each month's visit I was more and more curious about the upper levels of this huge home and its mysterious history. I even once tried to ask in a round-about way, but the good doctor obviously was uncomfortable with just the thought of an explanation, and she played the awkward moment off by pretending not to understand my words. I never asked again.

Down stairs she was a completely different woman. She was never shy about clarification or asking for help with the english word or phrase that would fit her story. For the first few months, we mainly spoke of her travels and things she had seen and done. I felt as if I was the first real person to listen to her in this way for many years. She was just as interested in me and hearing about my life, my past jobs, where I lived, and wanted hear all about my bride to be. She loved my stories about my old hitch hiking days especially, and said she could relate to suddenly being in a completely different environment and landscape. Still, there was always a line I could never cross. My visits always ended in a somber way when we came back downstairs and I would say good-bye at the front door.

## The Change

The summer heat was on the horizon, and my time with the doctor was coming to an end. I think she realized that her contract would be ending soon. Although she would love to have the companionship and verbal interaction, she knew that her practical side would win out in the end. Not needing my service any longer, she would cancel and once again go back to cutting coupons she didn't need and her lonely existence would remain hopelessly trapped on the first floor. I guess it was this realization, or maybe it was something I said, but the professor knew she needed a friend, someone she could trust. Being pragmatic perhaps, or just knowing she'd never willingly seek one out, she decided on the next best thing. On my next visit, I rang the bell. The 100 year old chimes echoed through the house and surprisingly I heard the doctor gleefully calling out as she rushed to the door. To my surprise she greeted me with a great big smile and sparkle in her eye. Then, up onto my chest jumped a beautiful six month old german shepherd pup lapping my face and welcoming me to his new home. The doctor was ecstatic and it was such a great moment. With a brief introduction, she quickly shut the door to keep the dog from running out into the busy street. The dog was just gorgeous and it was obvious that this grand lady had found her true friend and perhaps more importantly, hope for the future.

I was so happy for Dr. Muriez as I listened to her explain how she found the dog and the plans she had. She spoke with a joy in her voice that wasn't there even when she told some of her grandest stories or recalled some of the very important people she had met over the years. She had every detail mapped out right down to the dog bowls and where they'd be placed, to the corner of the yard where she was having a section fenced off just for the pup. She remembered that one of my previous jobs was building dog houses for a hardware store. The doctor asked if I could build one for her; she was thrilled when I said yes. Today's service visit was different from all the others. For the first time, I saw a woman who was thrilled with life and excited for the day. We made plans for me to come on the weekend to build the dog's new home. As I performed my service she happily spouted the details that she had carefully planned. But as happened each time before, when we made our way up the elegant staircase our conversation grew still. From the back yard we could hear the dog barking happily. We both forced a smile, but deep down I wondered if anything could fill this woman's empty void. At least now, there was a chance.

## At Contracts End

The contract was over and true to her nature the doctor had to let me and my service go. The dog grew fast and the last time I saw him he was very big but playful as ever. The dog house I built was well thought out,  just as everything was in Dr. Muriez' life. Made from cedar and insulated, it was one side job I was proud to do. We placed it on the side of a small out building in the back yard inside a chain link fence but visible from the drive. Dr. Muriez was a fine lady, and she paid me well above our agreed price for the work. I think it was a wedding present of sorts. Gifts were not part of her normal make up, so I think it served as a good excuse to give without breaking her beliefs. She also hand wrote a very nice commendation letter to my boss thanking me for my work. The letter was short and to the point, but knowing her the way I did, it was the equivalent of someone else writing a book. I still have the original to this day. Back then I remember reading it and wondering, wishing I knew more about the good doctor and the story behind the second and third floor. But my life went on and my bursting route and approaching marriage would not wait. So for that time, we both moved on so sure we would never again speak.

## The Call

It was six months or so after I had last seen the good doctor when I got the call at my home. It was the professor. She began speaking so fast, I could barely understand her even though I had gotten pretty good at it over the past year. I remember wondering how she got my number and I tried to make sense of what she was saying. I asked her to slow down and just tell me the problem. The phone went quiet for a few seconds; then Dr. Muriez began crying so very hard. It was as if flood gates of emotions that were held back for all these years came rushing out of her all at once. She said I was the only one she could think of calling, and the only one who would possibly care. She sobbed almost uncontrollably but she was finally able to convey the horrific story. She had only left the gate open for a moment when her beloved best friend bolted from his enclosure chasing a squirrel. The busy streets of Baltimore gave him no chance. I was devastated to hear the news and felt so bad for this grand lady, who it seemed that sadness would not leave alone.

We spoke for quite some time and we even shared a laugh about her pup and some of the funny things he'd do. I believe somewhere in the conversation her logical side came around to its usual place but brought along the loneliness she had lived with and accepted for so long. Feeling so sad for her, I offered to pray even though I knew this was something she abandoned years ago. Like the second and third floors, it was a line she would not cross. She stated politely but as a matter of fact, that this was not something she would ever consider. In her mind, she thought God had turned his back on her many years ago. Suddenly, it was as if we were again at the base of that grand staircase and the conversation was halted under a huge weight of sadness. As I hung up the phone I knew I would return to the fast and busy streets of life, but I'd be leaving her alone, once again, in her Hollow Mansion on 39th.

# The Worst Roach Infestation I've Ever Seen

### The Matrix

I love talking to the old veterans of pest control, and hearing their stories of horrific infestations that would make even Stephen King shudder. Roaches so bad that snow shovels were used to scoop them up after the service was done, rats and mice so thick that mattresses filled with their nests went flat once they were eradicated. Chemicals so powerful flies would drop in the neighbor's yard the minute they sprits around. Now for some of these old pros it's hard to know if after 30 years some of their stories weren't *just a little embellished.* But even if they were, every tall tale always has a little truth in it.

I've been around the bug world for about 25 years. (Where does the time go? Can you believe I'll be 29 next year?) I've seen some really wild stuff. I'm not sure if this story qualifies as a real horror flick that'll make you run for the door screaming, but it is definitely one of the worst I've seen and one I know I'll never forget.

### The Greeting

Sweat beaded on my forehead on this sweltering day. I patiently stood waiting at the door for the lady whom my office said was frantic and needed service right away. It seemed like it took forever. I wondered if this was just going to be another waste of time with phantom bugs, phobias or just exactly what the case would be. When the door finally opened I was greeted by a very large woman, whom I could tell immediately was blind. We exchanged greetings and she just stood there explaining her dilemma as I baked in the direct sun holding the screen door. I tried politely to make my way in but my body language was no help. She was a very sweet woman and so glad for some help but was unable to see me sweltering in the mid day sun. So I listened patiently and I could tell she was at her wits end. She called me "Mr. Jerry" and kept saying she just knew the bugs were bad, because she could *feel* them on her arms, legs, and even on her baby more frequently.

*"Mr. Jerry, I can't see, but I know they're here. I'm not a messy person, but I can't see. These roaches are getting the best of me. Can you please help me?" she said with desperation in her voice.*

When we finally started inside, I patiently followed behind her as she slowly moved along feeling her way. She frequently stopped to further describe her problem. Looking around, it didn't seem too out of hand. There were some roaches on the wall near the archway to the kitchen and a few on the floor of the living room. So thinking it wasn't that bad, I kept assuring her she was in good hands. I was struck how a woman who couldn't see seemed to know a lot of details of the roaches movements and hiding spots, which is something that those of us with good vision cannot always do. When she at last made it to the archway of the kitchen, she again stopped to talk. With her hand braced against the wall, three or four roaches were just hanging out past her finger tips but didn't seem to be bothered at all. It was so unbearably hot in this home, I was now sweating profusely and it didn't help we were moving at a snail's pace just to get to the room with all of the problems. She explained to me how she didn't have very much money and she couldn't run the air at all. She even held off on the pest control she needed because her baby's needs came first. She hoped some store bought chemicals would do the trick but the problem just got worse and worse.

Standing there and conversing wasn't helping my schedule much, but I liked this lady and truly wanted fix her problem. Of course anytime there's a child in need, it makes you want to try even harder to help. The longer I stood listening, the more movement caught my eyes. I began to see more and more roaches that were right in front of me the whole time. The carpet was dark brown but now as I acclimated myself, it was pretty easy to spot the female german roaches prancing across the shag with their oothecas bulging, ready to bust open with a new wave of filthy baby cockroaches. The archway too, had more activity, almost as if they heard us talking and they were curious to see the visitor. The heat was getting to the lady, so she had to sit on a nearby couch. Dozens of roaches scattered from beneath the cushions as she plunked down. I was finally beginning to see how bad this place was entrenched with roaches. What I took for an overly phobic woman at first, I now realized was someone in desperate need. For the first time, I wasn't sure I wanted to go into the kitchen but curiosity was getting the best of me if nothing else. What happened next, however, changed my inquisitiveness into a raging fire.

Suddenly, I had to get in that kitchen and kill every last roach in that house THAT DAY! It was almost as if I was Neo, star of the movie *Matrix,* in the scene where he saw his surroundings as they truly were for the first time. This sight opened my eyes and my lovely client could talk all she wanted, but I was going in.

# The Matrix Reloaded

In most of pest control work the thrill of the hunt is one of the most satisfying aspects. Finding clues that no one else can see and tracing down your prey is the most gratifying. Through that archway, I was sure there'd be no thrill on this day.

Over the years, I know I've gotten a lot less patient. It's not that a person disinterest's me with what they're saying, but in my mind, I've already put their clues and keywords together. At times I've got their problem solved long before they finish. Being a rookie back then, the clues were slow in mounting. For a lady who had no sight I was baffled at the terrible situation she described; that she had never witnessed in the traditional way. The roaches on the couch were still scurrying about. I wondered about how many she had pinned down and crushed when she all but collapsed on the cushion. She was in mid-sentence when her head jerked toward the arch way. She stopped talking. Her eyes made the movements as if she could see, but they were obviously lifeless and told her nothing.

*"C'mon baby," she said in a loving and caring tone. "C'mon out and meet Mr. Jerry, darling."*

I'm a sucker for kids and pets. Once in a while an adult will impress me too. From around the corner of the kitchen door way, the sound of tiny wheels half rolling and half scraping across the linoleum floor got louder. I guess that's what my lady heard. Out into the arch way came a beautiful baby girl in a walker, the kind with a tray and a seat so little ones could learn to walk and still enjoy a snack.

*"Help her onto the carpet, Mr. Jerry," she said, and I marveled how just by sound she knew exactly where the little one was.*

It was that moment when I leaned over to this cute smiling baby that horror reached up and grabbed my throat with a fist so tight I almost dropped to my knees. The baby, of course, had Cheerio's strewn about her tray. She also was eating some bread with peanut butter which was smeared all over her and her walker. What horrified me was there had to be at least 100 roaches climbing all over this defenseless little girl cashing in on this meal on wheels. She had roaches on her hands, in her hair, crawling all over the tray and there were even roaches on the floor trying to catch up to the moving bounty, so they could join in on the feast.

Mortified, I quickly brushed all of the roaches away and stomped and slapped them as they fell from the baby. The little one was surprised, I'm sure, by my sudden frantic outburst and began to cry. My sightless client didn't say a word, as if she knew I had come to a final realization of what she had been saying all along. I rolled the baby to her mother, grabbed my tool box and sprayer, and headed inside this roach job from hell.

## Raining Roaches

The kitchen was surprisingly bright, with white walls and appliances. The counter top was a porcelain material, like an old 1960 wash machine complete with the blue specks. The kitchen was free from clutter and not messy at all. There were roaches scattered about but I had seen much worse (or so I thought). Big Megatron Pest Control, for whom I worked, was a stickler for numbers but not really advanced on all the latest tools. Armed only with a B&G sprayer, duster filled with Drione and a couple of aerosol cans, I began the fight.

It didn't take long to start flushing the roaches, as their hiding spots were well marked with fecal matter that packed their cracks and lined the backs of every picture, appliance and anything that stayed in one place for any length of time. Pulling out the refrigerator unleashed a stampede of german roaches that scattered in every direction. As if some loud alarm went off through the population, the frantic roaches were running all over the kitchen trying to find a place to hide. Dusting is a fine art form I know, but I blew the max amount in every void, crack and crevice and was amazed at the ghost like roaches that careened out of their hiding spots covered in white and now blind by the dust, just like this lady that they had been torturing. German roaches in every stage of life were crawling up my legs looking for refuge and even scouring my equipment I set down hoping to find any untreated place to hide.

*"Sounds like it's raining in there Mr. Jerry," I heard from the living room which seemed like a whole world away.*

I hadn't been aware of the time that had passed, but I had been in the den of the lion for over an hour. Her words snapped me back to the present tense. She was right; I realized as I paused from my work and stood back in the archway of the door. Drenched from sweat I stood and gazed at this horrific sight. There was not one square inch that didn't have a roach in it twitching and writhing or running in circles. They were still falling off the ceiling hitting the 1960's amenities. Indeed, the small taps of each one hitting times the 1000's all at the same time, sounded like rain.

*"I'm sorry for the mess, hon. You'll have some cleaning to do," I said when I realized I couldn't do another thing in this 12 x 15 sized room.*

*"That's perfectly fine with me, Mr. Jerry," she told me with her now cute and happy baby on her lap, "I'll gladly send them to their final resting place–**outside for the trash man to take** , but it sounds like he's gonna need a bigger truck."*

*We both shared a laugh as I told her she had good hearing, and it's a good thing they're all dying, because I didn't have a drop of anything left.*

Not finished yet with this roach infestation straight from Hades and knowing I had thousands more to kill, I went out to my truck for more supplies. Like Neo in the movie, I was gonna go back inside to finish the rest of this nightmare-reloaded.

## The Show is Canceled the Matrix is Betrayed

I'm not one for taking breaks when I work because I like to just get in and get the job done. I'm famous for woofing my lunch down on the road and working in the pouring rain. Don't even think about calling me during a job! Somehow, in this case I decided to take a few minutes and sit in my non air conditioned apartment on wheels (thanks, Megatron Pest Company) and just try to take in what I had just witnessed and what I was about ready to get back into.

It was blazing hot in the Baltimore sun as I reloaded my weapons. I planned in my mind the rest of my assault. Now, I was so far behind on my schedule, I feared the wrath of my service manager if he got too many calls from waiting clients. I was also really low on supplies and still needed some for the rest of the day. I did find what I needed and also a half can of Aero Term. That stuff could knock a bull on its butt so it was time to finish the job. My strategy changed from all out chemical warfare to one of stealth and economy treatments (whatever the hell that means–remember I was a rookie). The heat was stifling as I re-entered the house, worse than being outside. I couldn't imagine having to live in these conditions.

*"Man, O man, Mr. Jerry, you sure are working hard today. I do so appreciate that God has sent you to me," my lovely client said. I knew she meant it, and it was her sincerity and strength that urged me on to do whatever it took to make her life better in my own little way.*

I asked her to move to another room and I began working at a furious pace knowing I had stops waiting for me. The couch was disgusting. Indeed, I found just as many dead roaches squashed in the cushions as I did alive. Flipping the thing over revealed hundreds more, and as they tried to scatter I judiciously sprayed them all with my aerosol of death and my now refilled B&G set on fan spray. I wasn't smart enough to fire up the vacuum that was perched in the corner and save chemicals but she was. She said when she used the attachments *she could feel the roaches* being sucked through the hose. I was amazed at her ability to sense things I couldn't dream of and realized I had several handicaps that she did not. My lady was talking again, but not as much as in the beginning. She let me know she had a hard life but was thankful none the less. Being blind might seem like a handicap but I sensed she had no room for people to pity her. She rarely asked for help but these roaches really got the best of her this time.

## The Beginning Of The End

As I got further from the kitchen, the problem subsided immensely. This was a three story row home. With the population explosion in the kitchen, I was pleasantly surprised there wasn't much at all in the basement or upstairs. I worried that she might complain I rushed through the rest of the house. But I declared the job done, and explained what she could expect in the coming month. Being curious, I took one last look in the kitchen and couldn't believe the carnage I had wrought. It was a sea of dead roaches almost all on their backs. Most were still twitching or running around in a tight circle. The thought of the little one crawling around while mama tried to clean was something I couldn't bear. I couldn't leave this lady who couldn't see with such a mess fearing she may fall on the slick of dead roaches. It only took a short time, but I swept up all the bugs, grabbed the vacuum, and did what I could on the thick living room carpet. It wasn't perfect, but at least this mostly self-reliant person could get what was left.

# No Good Deed Goes Unpunished

I've seen so many things in my career that I don't know if anything shocks me anymore. Just when I say that, this profession of mine will just throw me for a loop. Megatron Pest Control, who was my employer, demanded one year contracts. They came down hard on salesmen whose deals fell through (especially when it happened in the early stages). The penalty for early cancelations was called a 'charge-back', meaning any money the salesman gained from the sale was taken out of his next commission check. The formula was complicated to say the least but it was an 'out' for the sales weasel to blame the service guy. He could at least get the commission for the clean out fee which amounted to about $10.00 and sometimes he could salvage more if it was proven to be faulty service from the technician. That rarely worked but it was tried in this instance. When I called my customer for her first regular visit, she explained she couldn't afford it, and had to cancel her contract. As mandated I asked her why and she explained she wasn't satisfied.

I was a bad tech for a day or two and had to listen to my manager explain the virtues of retaining customers, as well as endure dirty looks from the sales guy who lost a whopping $45.00. But they didn't see the wonderful lady I saw, who tried to get ahead, the woman with a baby who could barely make ends meet. Her life was something so many would pity but she'd have none of it. She did what she had to do for her baby, who was her pride and joy, her reason for life. She knew these insects were bad news. She told me many times that she prayed to God to send her someone who could solve her problem and give her just a little help. In the end, it didn't matter what my boss said or the salesman thought, because I knew she couldn't afford any more than the initial visit. Truth be told some 25 years later, *I'm the one who told her **how to cancel.*** To be even more truthful, it took me three more months to solve her problem and clean up all her roaches, and yes, I did it as a side job. I never accepted a dime. My apologies to Megatron pest Control.

# Silent Signs of Pest Control

It is just another day on my very busy route as I make my way across town to a very large high rise apartment complex. There's really nothing unique (well almost nothing) about the building itself. The roaches and mice scurry in between the walls, back and forth, just as they do in any of the other 1000's of similar buildings I've done. I use the same techniques, the same chemicals and struggle with the same challenges of sanitation, exclusion and education I always do. But this building in particular was, with all its similarities, completely different and much more demanding than all of the regular buildings combined.

Checking in, I always had a log with *special concerns* (complaints) to go along with the regularly scheduled units. The 'super' liked me, just gave me my badge, and let me have at it even though he was supposed to come along. He was a very busy man and he liked how I handled myself. He said if I could keep his people happy, then he was happy with me. I almost always started at the highest floor and worked my way down but even if the elevator might be filled with residents, it was always a quiet ride. Coming to my first apartment I'd push the button to signal my arrival, but never once would hear the occupants inside saying, "Come in, or who is it?" the way one would expect. In fact the doorbell made no sound at all but rather simply triggered a light inside. Many times I just had to wait, not knowing if they were home or not. Skipping that unit and using the excuse 'no one answered the door' would never wash in this place. Once inside the apartment, my seemingly normal job took a big twist. Although no words were ever spoken, I soon learned the value of communication and a lot about some people I might not have ever given the time before. Oh, I also learned a lot about myself.

## Silent Service

The entire apartment complex was for people who could not hear or speak. At first it was very difficult to treat their homes because I could not understand what they were trying to communicate. They did try to mouth the words. Their hands went a mile a minute with sign language to one another, but I felt like a foreigner from a far-away land. My first few visits were so frustrating because as it is with most clients, they had preferences of where they might not want spraying, or in vain tried to tell me where they saw a bug but I wasn't getting it. Their guttural moans always made me feel like I was doing something terribly wrong. At times they smacked their lips with the back of their hand, or raked their hands up their bellies with an annoyed look on their face, which told me I was close to stepping over a line. I must admit this was a little unnerving and I was frustrated that my usually excellent communication skills were now my biggest hindrance.

## A Super Sign

The super was a really nice guy and pulled me aside one day. He showed me a few signs that helped turn everything around. I already guessed what the belly rub was, and he laughed and said as long as it's not just one hand that goes all the way to the forehead you'll be alright. He showed me the sign for "bug, mouse, thank you and show me" as well as some others that, sadly I've long since forgotten. This was so great and opened up a whole other world to me. My service immediately got better. What's more, it alleviated my customer's frustrations. Now I was getting smiles and even laughter when I would attempt to sign something which I'm sure made no sense.

Most importantly, I was able to shake off my fears and judgments and see these folks for who they were, PEOPLE. Just folks enjoying life and getting by like anybody else, with many of the same problems, setbacks, and challenges that we all have. Sure, some might say they had a tougher hill to climb, but after a while I couldn't tell you that at all. These were truly happy people, some of the best customers I ever had. They didn't feel sorry for themselves nor look for any special treatment. If anything, I felt disadvantaged for not being fluent enough to get to know them better. I was able to rejoice with them in births of babies, graduations, jobs, and even the satisfaction of finally ridding their homes of pests. I was very sad when I learned I was transferring to another route and would no longer be seeing these great people on a regular basis. The last sign I learned was one of appreciation because by now, most of my clients knew I was leaving. I eagerly gave it back. With BOTH palms toward your face you extend your hands forward in a mini semi-circle way as if blowing a kiss. This was the sign of 'thankful', and it's exactly the way I felt for my time with all of them.

# The Secret Sex Tapes Of An Exterminator

I've always tried to lead a quiet and honest life. But, I am human and prone to mistakes just like anyone else. I'd like to think of my readers as a faithful family, there to pick me up when I fall short and always willing to hear me out before they come to judgment. In turn, I promise to leave my stones on the ground and not hurl any unwarranted negatives in your direction as well. Sometimes just telling the story can cleanse the soul. I find it so liberating to share with you, my loyal readers, all of my experiences good or bad. This is my story about some tapes that I had no idea existed, but I fear will one day surface.

In my days of the commercial route, I saw so many unique things and learned a lot about how everyday things were manufactured, produced, packaged and shipped.  I saw anything from styrofoam cups, to hot dogs, and everything in between. The machines that people invent to accomplish these tasks are also amazing. Some might even qualify as the eighth wonder of the world and you get to see it all in the wonderful world of pest control. Not all my stops were so exciting and glamorous however; some were downright mundane and repetitive. On those services, I muddled through like a good tech does, but I wanted more. The excitement and thrills that a 20 acre rat infested warehouse complex could bring, or riding up a conveyor belt through the floors of an 11 story building. I had so many interesting and challenging jobs, that when a simple office building or converted house that was now a business came my way; it was kind of a let-down. I was always looking to spice things up.

## The Mundane Disguise

One such account came my way which no amount of training could have properly prepared me for. The salesman must have been pretty good, because the price he got for this non de-script office building with a small warehouse attached was actually pretty high. Entering the building, the receptionists knew I was coming. She had me sign in, but then simply said, "Do your thing." I was left alone to wander through the office area treating the target pest of ants. As offices go, it was very nice, but hardly anybody was around. Leather couches were in each office and on the doors the executive names were embossed in gold on the rich dark wood. The 'suits' dining area was really nice. Real chairs and tables and the silverware looked like Mom's best set that she kept in a separate drawer for company. The bathrooms were deluxe complete with company logos on the designer made hand towels. Even the broom closet was so well kept with all the most modern vacuums and equipment. The big conference room was paneled with real wood and Lay-Z-Boy chairs surrounded this huge oak table that was probably hand made. A very large cabinet housed a bank of TV's and the wet bar was fully stocked. "Hmm, maybe there was more to this account than I had figured, I thought to myself. Just what do they manufacture?" It has to be something very profitable and I headed out to the warehouse where I was sure to get my answer.

## The Lilly White Warehouse

Like I said, this wasn't a big building. The warehouse was no bigger than the front office area. It was very clean, well lit and busy with at least eight to ten workers all scurrying about. Each employee had a name tag and wore a white jump suit. They weren't really the friendliest lot. Except for a fork lift (that was clean as a whistle), there was only single pallets on the floor with just enough of their product to fill it. As I normally do, I started to the right and began looking for ants and treating as I go. The first couple pallets were no big deal, just some weird contraption that looked like a fish tank pump in boxes. I began to wonder just how this place stayed in business. The rest of the stock however, gave me my answer in unmistakable clarity. My body began to tighten up as my curiosity left and shock took over.

This warehouse was a depot of sorts for adult toys. In this small simple warehouse, their stock included everything that you could possibly imagine. I'm sure the employees got a kick out of watching me turn as white as a ghost at first, only then turn red from embarrassment as I passed each pallet with it's different kind of, eh, hmm, manufactured goods? I'm really not sure if I saw any ants out there, I don't remember. I think I went into a confused daze, but somehow made it back to the door that would take me back to the ornate office area which I wondered about so much. This account with its unassuming structure was definitely out of the boring category, but not in the way in which I was used to.

## The Tapes

I actually had another account added to my route around the same time (same company?). It was very similar. This one was in the city but was a converted house. However, it was set up as a call center for a community 'hot line' as well. I'm sure at a $1.99 per minute they had no trouble whatsoever paying for all of their fancy silverware. It was the same sort of deal as the warehouse, they left me to do my job and I just wandered around treating what I could. I was oh so careful not to spray any of their, eh-em, goods as well. Any employees present were always professional, dressed in white jump suits and pretty much stayed to themselves. As with a lot of accounts in those days, the iron clad contract kept them customers for the year and then they'd cancel in the 12th month. These two were no different.

It was probably the 11th month that I learned a lesson that I really didn't need, but has stuck with me ever since, and a lesson I teach to anyone I train. I was in the big conference room with the bank of TVs and to my surprise, one of the 'suits' was in there eating his lunch with every set on. He thanked me for my work and promised he'd call if he ever needed service again. He said the main reason he would call again was because all year he had watched me in both 'stores' with his hidden cameras on his many sets. "Theft is a big problem in my business" he stated as a matter of fact, and he said nothing more. As I looked at the video bank, I saw every nook of the warehouse and each employee was in plain sight. It had never dawned on me to take anything anyway, but I had no idea there were any cameras and never saw them at all during the year. Well, it was kind of hard to focus to be honest.

Well, there you have it, a confession of sorts. I'm sure my every move was captured and stored somewhere on a server in a place I never saw. I know you'd have never thought in a million years- The Bug Doctor himself would be caught up in such a thing. I can only imagine the scandal, so if you don't mind let's just keep this one, 'in the family.' I just dread the day if and when these images come out, and I'm exposed and will forever be known as the exterminator caught on tape.

# My 25th Anniversary with My Wife and Mrs. Adams

It's hard to imagine that I've been doing anything for 25 years, but in a little less than a month I'll hit that wonderful milestone with the greatest woman God has put on this earth. About the same time, I'll have another anniversary pass that brings back fond memories, and is just one more reason why I love my job so much.

In my early route running days, I had the area that surrounded Memorial Stadium where the then 'contending' Baltimore Orioles played. It was as if the stadium was the center of the universe and on each side was a whole different planet. The main street ran in a circular pattern directly around the aging structure, then others fractioned off into their own little galaxies. There were the upscale homes and those of privilege that lived just past the first base line. Beyond second base and the outfield were the hard working middle class. This area came complete with its own version of a *Cheers* type bar and many thriving, but small businesses. Rounding third, you found those who were struggling but too proud to give in. By the time you came to home plate, you wondered just how these people ever made it through a day. Mrs. Adams lived behind home base .

### First Impressions

I remember getting my work for the day.  Mrs. Adams was set as a 'new start,' and seeing the address I figured this initial service was going to be a whopper. Pulling up to her row home in this once proud neighborhood, I figured I was in for a rough roach job or maybe rats. I was startled by the lady who answered the door in her thick and shabby wool coat and a hat fit for a Russian house wife in a Siberian winter. She stood all of 5 feet tall and her grizzled face and hairy mole took me by surprise. She couldn't walk very well. Her poodle was very excited and his leash tangled around her feet. I noticed she wore two different kinds of shoes and both looked at least 30 years old. As she made her way to the kitchen table to sit, she explained to me about her problems with some bugs she just couldn't get rid of. She had bugs alright, and by the looks of things, I was going to need every bit of the year-long contract to which she had agreed to.

As I worked she just talked and I felt she was glad to have somewhat of a captive audience. I admit I didn't hear much on that first time out, but was instead astonished by the amount of 'stuff' she had collected all throughout the home. Stacks of newspapers just about filled the front family room. The kitchen was filled with old boxes and bags of out dated foods. Piles of clothing, boxes, files and just about anything you could imagine filled this home, leaving only a network of pathways to get from one area to the next. I was at a loss of just how to treat this place and no book or video I watched during my training could have prepared me for this. I decided to use dusts where I could and resorted to Baygon bait in spots I was sure the dog couldn't get to. Liquids were out for now because there was absolutely no place to spray where the liquid wouldn't get soaked up by a box, paper, or article of clothing. This was going to be a long year, but something about this lady made me want to try and really help her in a way that wasn't in any training manual.

## A Diamond In The Rough

The next month came and Mrs. Adams was very happy to see me. *"You killed a lot of bugs,"* she said in her gruff marbled voice. She again made her way to the kitchen table and began to talk as I performed my work. For this service, I decided to ask her if I could remove old food boxes and the like from the kitchen so I could treat more effectively. She hesitated and wondered out loud, *"What if I need these things?"* I explained that the bugs have already ruined her supplies, but I'd save what I could. She finally agreed. With the back door open, I began carting box after box and endless bags of unopened foods out to the alley. Roaches tried frantically to make their escape, the weevils and beetles scurried for cover as I dislodged their cozy harborage and all the while I was listening to Mrs. Adams tell me about her life story. She was a very interesting woman who had worked most of her life in factories downtown. She asked me of my life and where I had been. She seemed genuinely interested when I relayed a few humdinger stories of my own. *"Ain't safe for a boy your age to be hitch hiking all over the country,"* she exclaimed when I told her how it was I ended up in Baltimore. *"You came here to teach the Bible? They don't need the Good Word in Oregon?"* She smiled when I exclaimed that maybe God sent me here just for her. I continued to work and she just went right on talking and filling me in on everything that had ever happened in her life.

As each month passed, the infestation level went way down, but Mrs. Adams drew the line on things I couldn't take out of the house. By this time, I actually had places I could treat. The dog was happier than ever because he had room to run, well sort of. At least it was better than the back and forth in the narrow pathways that he had before. I had all but ridden her of the german roaches and we hadn't seen a stored product pest in months. I came to enjoy my time with this wonderful woman. Her heart was so big and she saw the positive in almost everything. Even though she looked like she had been living on the streets for years, she had a great wisdom about her. She taught me so much about life and people just by her thoughtful remarks. Although I'm sure life had kicked her down quite a bit, you would never know it by speaking with her. Even though she rarely changed clothes and I'm sure even rarer, took a shower, this lady was an eloquent queen and someone that I came to adore.

**Contracts End New Life Begins**

The end of her contract came all too soon. Mrs. Adams explained to me something I already knew. She would have to cancel because she couldn't afford the $22.00 a month, but she wished I would come back and visit. I was all too happy to say yes, but we both knew that my busy route wouldn't give me much time. So I agreed to come once a month on a Saturday. It was also about this time that I told her that my lovely girlfriend had finally said yes and I would be getting married in June. Mrs. Adams was the one who gave me the greatest words of wisdom six months previous when I first asked my steady to marry me and she said no. "*Good for her,*" she cackled in her famous raspy voice, "*Now there's a gal who has her head on straight. You stick with this gal, and it'll work out fine."* She never minced words. In her gruff way, she put life in such a wonderful light that I have seldom seen since.

I continued to stop by but it was getting harder to make the time. On one sad visit I found her crying because her dog had died. I buried him in a non de-script grave in the back yard and I believe a big part of her went right along with her tiny best friend. In June of 1985, I visited and found Mrs. Adams quiet and more intent than I had ever seen her before. She had slowly gone down hill with the death of her dog, her loyal and trusted friend.  It was sad to watch a woman who had taken all of life's heart aches and bounce back each time, only now to be broken and tired. She was however, excited for me and my wedding only a few weeks away. Although I pleaded with her many times to come and even brought her an invitation, she refused each time. She made excuses of not having anything to wear and for the first time got a bit angry with me when I pressed her on the issue. She finally broke down and cried and admitted that she had not been out of her home for many years due to a –well, let's just say embarrassing problem that she couldn't control. As I told her I understood she grabbed my arm and gently sobbed and told me what our time together had meant to her. Her hand was ice cold and leathery, but her grip was tight. I assured her I'd be back and I was looking forward to seeing her once I returned from my honeymoon. She made a weak attempt at a smile and pulled something from her sweater pocket and stuffed it in my hand and tightened her grip so I could not pull away. I could tell it was money. I immediately balked and told her she should keep it. With her other hand she touched my face, with tears in her eyes she told me how much this meant to her, how she wanted to bless my life the way I had hers. When she loosened her hand I sheepishly put the wad in my pocket. I gave her a big hug and headed for home.

## The Honeymoon's Over

That month was a busy one to say the least. I had family in from Oregon and all the hectic things to deal with that a wedding brings along. It wasn't until a few days later when my fiancée and I were doing laundry that we found the money in my pocket and we were completely blown away. It was a wad alright, as big as your fist, all one dollar bills. I figure Mrs. Adams had been saving for months and probably went without, which is something she always talked about almost as if it were a source of pride. When we were done counting the bills it added up to $150.00. This might as well have been a million dollars considering where it came from. I tried to call Mrs. Adams before the wedding to thank her, but having watched her many times just let the phone ring off the hook and never answer, I wasn't at all concerned when she didn't pick up.

Our wedding day was a glorious event. Our lives together had just started with the promise of great things. Once home and back to work, I made it a point to stop back by Mrs. Adams home on an unscheduled day. I knew she'd want to hear of the great day and all about the wedding. Sadly, her home was locked up and there were no lights or signs of Mrs. Adams. A neighbor poked out and told me that Mrs. Adams had died. I felt like I had just been punched in the stomach and couldn't catch my breath. I was mad at the neighbor who suddenly knew what was going on but never lifted a finger to help in all these years. I felt helpless because Mrs. Adams had no family, there was no one I could contact and nothing I could do. Making my way to my tiny little bug truck, I cried as I pulled away and left her home for the very last time.

It's been 25 years since I met this fine lady and I still think of her often. Her way of doing things and her demeanor may have turned off most anybody else, but for me she was a beautiful woman who understood life in a way very few people do. It's getting to be that time of year again, when I celebrate the wonderful life I've made with my wife who is the greatest woman God put on this earth. It is also a time when I think back about another wonderful lady who made such a great impression on me and one whom I'll never forget. I'm sure one day I'll see Mrs. Adams again and this time I'm sure things will be much different. I can't wait to see her in her brand new coat and matching shoes. To once again hear her 'life lesson stories' and that great cackled laugh. To hear such uncommon wisdom from the most unlikely source. To just sit and talk for hours at the kitchen table in her brand new home. A beautiful mansion just for her, down the first base line. God Bless you Mrs. Adams.

# My Time Behind Bars And What I Learned About Pest Control

Looking up over the 16 foot wall with the razor wire glimmering in the sun, you see the clouds floating by and the birds freely going back and forth. Taunting you, they flit with ease right over the rampart that holds you in as they chirp with a gleeful refrain. It's different inside these walls, much different. You can go nowhere without eyes upon you and a pat down. Locking doors make an unmistakable sound of which you have no control whatsoever whether it opens or shuts. Inside those walls time has a different meaning. If you accomplish a task, great; if you don't, oh well. You've always got time to talk and so you do a lot of it. You're never quite sure if the lines you're fed are true or just made up. Embellishment is so common place here because of the endless hours inmates have to just think and dream, hoping for the time you get to hear those locking doors for the last time.

**Everyones An Expert**

In the real world, getting your pest control license requires time, experience, money and study. But, in the finite wisdom of the powers that be, a system has been set up that allows a guard or maintenance employee for the cost of $25.00, to take a 15 question test and have a license. Albeit limited, this neophyte is allowed to apply chemicals in otherwise forbidden fashion. To say the least, this is a major short cut of the norm. This then cuts the hard working entrepreneur out of a gig. It saves the tax payers money, I guess, and permits even an inmate to run the halls with a sprayer hosing down the concrete walls at their base. In the real world you trained for years to learn the pest control craft. Behind these walls  make one wrong swipe and you could be asking for trouble that no $25 dollar quiz could prepare you for. In my time behind lock and key, I saw so many strange things and met some of life's most peculiar people. Not a one was guilty of course and everyone had a comment as I went by with my sprayer. I learned quickly to keep my thoughts to myself.

The buildings were constantly in a state of upgrade by the inmates which I think helped keep them sane and the pests to a minimum. Even in the kitchen where you'd bet your bottom dollar infestations would be out of control, it was never that bad. Still, german roaches had to adapt to their surroundings. Nests were located farther apart than what you would see in a civilian restaurant. Out of necessity they would huddle by the hundreds in the smallest cracks that somehow still existed after all the layers of caulk and paint were applied over the years. While moisture is the highest priority to so many insects and pests, the roaches in these brick and stainless steel institutions took what they could get and learned how to go with less.

**Never Let Your Guard Down**

In the cells of certain individuals you learned quickly NOT to spray. The roaches were a source of 'interest' and kept the prisoner occupied in a sick sort of twisted way. There was really no use for aerosols or extra equipment, as I'm sure the guards feared that something might be stolen and used for a weapon. Even your hand pump sprayer was opened and checked every once in a while just to keep you on your toes and a reminder of the possibility of getting caught while smuggling something through the compound. This also happened every time the bug truck was brought inside the gates. Fearing an inmate would hold his breath and hide in your Dursban mix, they used a special stick to probe the 100 gallon tank. I felt guilty for the longest time like they didn't trust me, but after a few years I got use to the guards exploring my equipment and their ever watchful eyes.

Mice were extremely hard to deal with, because baits and snap traps were never allowed. Glue boards were the compound favorite. I carried two boxes of 72 on me with each service. As I'd pass through an office building or guard shack I was always asked for some. I knew those boards were going home with the guard and not on the floor behind the desk. In desperation, I learned how to cut the boards in half using a soapy pair of scissors and this kept me stocked up on most days.

**A Complex Service**

There were all sorts of buildings in the compound, chapels, libraries, sheds, office buildings and even a commissary. Not too much unlike an exterminator would have to deal with on the outside. In most prisons, (I've been in a few), the commissary and the guard shacks were the only air conditioned structures inside the fence. In the heat of the summer you'd have to plan your route so you'd hit one just about the time the heat would be too much. Being friendly with the guard always helped to buy you a few extra minutes inside so you'd get a chance to cool down. I'd usually pull out a few 'uncut' glue boards just for him. Inside these walls, you did what you had to do, even if it was a bit shady.

The worst places to treat were always the cell blocks. It started before you even entered their building. You could hear inmates calling out to you from their windows as you walked across the grounds. Sudden pleas to the guards about their huge problems of gnats or spiders rang out. Walking down the halls the clamor was deafening. It was wise to take care and not get any spray on a magazine or bed roll because you'd never hear the end of it. It's amazing what these jail birds would have packed in their 6×10 rooms. About the only safe place to spray was around the solid stainless steel commode and maybe, a sprits along the entry. DC (disciplinary confinement) was the worst of the worst. You would only be called in there for head lice, and though you try to explain that pest control would do no good, you had no choice but to spray. Always accompanied with two or more guards, they'd lead the trouble maker out to avoid any close encounter. The prisoner had the huge initials "DC" on his back and everybody took notice. The cement block bed with its two inch thick plastic mattress was all that was in these rooms. These bad boys were famous for 'fecal matter' paintings; one would just wonder what the hell was in their heads and just how they got their 'art', so high on the wall.

## My Sentence Crossed State Lines

In Baltimore (yes, I spent time behind the wall there too), I learned quite a bit about bird control. We were allowed to use a corn based bait called Avitrol on the roofs of only the farthest buildings, but things like' Hot Feet' or 'Roost No More' were our main tools. This caulk like substance was messy but it kept the pigeons off the ledges but you had to use it sparingly since they limited what you could carry. Roof tops were perhaps the most scrutinized place on the grounds and before you could step foot on a roof, it had to cleared with all the towers. Early on in my, eh-em, career, I bounded out an open roof door eager for some light but was abruptly grabbed by the neck and quickly hauled back in. It was explained to me that guards have orders to shoot to kill in any case of unauthorized personnel on a roof top. I was probably in the sites of one or two of the guards' scopes- that never happened again.

Juvenile prisons were for me the absolute worst (hey, you gotta start early in this career). I saw more fights and disrespect in those halls than I ever did in the adult system. The girls were so bad that they were almost always lined up against one wall while I would be on the other side spraying. There were a few times I actually feared for my life as conversations turned to heated accusations and loud verbal threats. I learned early on that my mouth was to stay shut and I carried that tradition on throughout all the penal systems I entered.

**Freedom**

Pest control inside a prison was so much different than anything in the free and open air. You really had to be diplomatic with as few of words as possible and learn how to be effective with very limited tools. I was actually saddened the day I got the news that I had treated my last cell and that I was released. You see, my hard labor and time behind bars was never as a result of any crime. I was only a contractor who won the bid, but was finally let go when some lucky guard answered nine out of 15 questions right and was allowed to take my place. I've never been back but some facilities now realize the importance of professional service and are more flexible with their budgets, so I guess I could put in another bid if I wanted to. For me though, I've had enough of that life and I'm now on the straight and narrow serving the outside world. Although I learned a lot, hearing the sound of the big metal door lock behind me that day, was the last time I ever wanted to be behind bars.

# Wednesday Morning Hot Dogs And The Dark Abyss

It was Wednesday again; I was off to my weekly 5:15 am visit to a once massive meat processing facility that through the years had dwindled down its services to just manufacturing hot dogs. It was bitterly cold outside as I reached into my tool box and pulled out the only chemical I was allowed to use inside the plant. I grabbed two cans of Aero term, which I think was just pure pyrethrin but man, was that stuff powerful! It was not much warmer when I got inside and the whipping noise of the wind was quickly replaced with the roar of fork lifts, the scraping of stainless steel shovels, and men shouting at each other. No one was shouting in anger mind you, it was just the way they spoke to one another over the loud steady noises.

I whisked past the U.S.D.A. office which I was told I would never want to be called in to. For that to ever happen would mean I've done something very terribly wrong and heads would be rolling. Checking in, I found my pest sighting log and scanned for any new entries. As usual there was nothing written at all except for some doodling from a bored supervisor. It's been that way for a while, but I always knew when the U.S.D.A. man had emerged from his office for his surprise inspections. Because suddenly, there were dates and notes all scribbled down in a very haphazard way. So off I went wandering through the factory but I found myself looking around more than any actual treating.

For this account, my main job was inspections, but not of the entire plant. I did all the break rooms, locker areas, docks, offices, and then once per month–*the subterranean levels.*

When I first started the account I was lost, my training up to that point was to spray first and ask questions later. It took me awhile to get used to just inspecting but soon I got very good at spotting problems just by looking. I'd use the Aero term to flush out any suspect areas and that stuff not only flushed them, it fried them. Once in a blue moon I'd get some roaches behind the time clock but that was about it. The men working the plant were all very nice, I guess. *"Going down to the basements?"* they'd yell trying to compete with all the noise bouncing off the cement walls. They reminded me of Pauley from the movie *Rocky*. I know they were just trying to unnerve me so I'd just smile and scream back, *"Inspector's got 'you' doing it this month,"* and I'd be on my way. At Christmas time, they gave me a present and they were all grinning from ear to ear when they told me how they all pitched in. It was a stainless steel mesh glove and it was from the days when the plant was a full blown slaughter house. The cutters used the glove to keep all their fingers in tact from the sharp knives. They told me I should wear it for protection during my monthly descent. *"It might come in handy in case a rat attacks you"* they exclaimed. They were all wearing $h*t eating grins as I tried so hard to be stone faced but I don't think I was fooling anyone, especially myself.

# Not A Fan Of The Recipe

Seeing how hot dogs were made was both fascinating and gross. The meat was like some puree or pudding that they hauled around in what looked like stainless steel dumpsters. They actually shoveled it with stainless steel snow shovels right off the cement as it poured out of a large industrial blender, the slurry mix was a puke pink color as it plopped out onto the cold floor. The goo went into another machine that shot it into a long clear tube. There it was cut into six inch lengths, tied off and hung on conveyor racks that slowly meandered through garage sized ovens. For lack of a better description, it looked like the John Wayne Bobbitt tribute memorial. I couldn't believe people actually ate these disgusting things. It took me over a year before I could even think about eating a hot dog after seeing that. However, once I got used to it and relented to the prodding of the workers, I was picking them straight from the strings as they came through the massive ovens fully cooked. Funny what the mind goes through.

Like I said it was an easy job, and I came to learn I was there more for fulfilling a time requirement than anything else. Sure I kept things in check but nothing really got out of hand roach wise. There was however, a huge challenge to this job and I still get chills thinking about it to this day. You see, once per month I not only brought in my Aero term but I also brought in a huge bucket of rat bait. I wasn't allowed to put anything on the upper levels mind you, that would be to easy-no no no. This rat bait was destined for an area of the plant, that besides me and any other previous pest control technician, hadn't been seen with human eyes for over 30 years.

# The Dreaded Day

Oh, 3:30 am comes early but on this day especially, it's all too soon. I just wanted to roll over and keep my hand on the snooze button and hold it until dinner time. This was the day that no matter how I prepared my mind or imagined happy thoughts, I knew I would be faced with bubbling fears that would test me to the limits. As I drove the beltway and made my way onto Wilkins Boulevard, I was not alone on the roads. In this busy city, life starts early and people were hustling to their jobs. Most however, get to go to a nice warm well lit office, while I would soon be faced with one of man's most primordial fears.

My first stop was a hospital kitchen which I also did every week. That in itself is a story but I couldn't drag my feet because my schedule was so tight. It was hard to keep my mind on this job knowing what lie ahead. The hot dog factory was waiting and only blocks away, so my truck didn't even warm up from the frigid cold before I pulled into the dark factory parking lot. On this dreaded day, I not only brought in my Aero term but a five pound bucket of apple flavored rat bait and two flash lights along with a huge pit in my stomach. The jeers started immediately as I walked through the huge plastic curtains that separate the dock from the outside world. *"Ah, LOOK who's going downstairs today!"* they yelled in a loud and joyful tone. Like dogs barking from yard to yard, their loud calls were heard from other rooms and the news was passed throughout the facility over the loud roar of fork lifts and machinery.

## Torment

My regular service would go as planned but I couldn't tarry or put off the inevitable. By this time, I had talked myself into a bravado that I hoped would last. *"How many floors are you gonna get today?"* someone yelled, and as if a Vegas ticker tape was up on the wall, the men started placing their bets. I just smiled with fake confidence and held up five fingers. All I got was looks of gleeful disbelief and increased betting odds as the men cackled like a pack of laughing hyenas.

With bucket in hand and flashlights in each pocket, I came to the door that I have been dreading all month. Three or four of my tormentors always snuck away from the noise filled plant and accompanied me to the quietest room in the building. The door creaked opened to an old metal stairway and one could see the remnants of a once busy slaughter house. This very large room had lights albeit dim and I made my way down the stairs. The room was filled with old metal rails that made pathways like the entry to the rides at Disney to keep the people in line. These pathways weren't for people however and they all ended at medieval looking stations where the poor animals met their fate and conveyor belts took them from there. Rust stains ran down the once shiny metal and looked as if it were blood from years ago. This is when my bravado began to wane.

## The Grip Of Fear

The job was simple - walk and throw rat bait. No one cared about proper placement or text book technique. Of course, 'Pauley' and his friends called out from the stairway, played with the lights and giggled like school kids each time the room went pitch dark. In each corner were a set of stairs going down. Making my way to the farthest one, I briskly headed down so as not to alert the boys in the hair nets that they were getting to me. As I descended to the floor below, my comfort gave way as their laughter and the light grew faint. This level, as well as the others I dared to endure were completely dark and had no electricity. My flashlight was all the comfort I had but even it caused some of the most horrific shadows as I made my way through the dark. Suddenly, I longed for the deafening roar of the fork lifts and the scraping shovels that moved the pink goo. I bumbled my way to about the middle of the darkness and just threw the bait blocks as far as I could. The hard bait bounced off of the walls and God only knows what kind of metal death machines. That noise alone put my mind in so many different places. Was that a rat, a mouse, or was there someone else down here moving in the darkness and making their way over to get me? I tried to control my thoughts but by now they were growing louder than any fork lift. Turning about, I made my way back to the staircase. I was thankful for what little light came down through the stairway opening.

It would take a few minutes of letting my eyes adjust, half in the dim light of the upstairs but facing the utter and complete darkness below. So much fear and dread and I had only gone down one floor. Setting my mind, I made my way down the next flight and the weak light from up above became almost non-existent. My strategy was again to go to the middle of the dark abyss and throw bait but my feet weren't so eager to carry me. The darkness this far down seemed to weigh a ton and I could manage no more than a few yards away from the stairs that led to my escape. Instead I just threw the blocks of bait even harder. By now every noise and image was magnified 100 x. I felt as if I was in the middle of the most horrible Alfred Hitchcock movie ever made. My back up flashlight would clang on some unknown object and I would jump thinking someone was behind me for sure. Imagined or not, horrific noises filled my head and the shadows from my light took on a life of their own. I saw angry figures that stalked me and hovered over my every move. I'm sure it was freezing in this part of the building but my trembling body was sweating profusely. I could no longer talk myself in to going any further. I doubted if I could even find the stairs and my way out. Panic filled my mind as I finally bumbled my way to the staircase because by now I was sure I'd never make it out of here alive. I sprinted up the metal stairs chased by my own footsteps hollow echo bouncing of the rust stained walls. With my heart about to burst out of my chest my shaking hand made my flashlight beam appear like that of a strobe light and nothing seem to fit in time as I sprinted up the metal stairs. Only when I made it back up to the first sub level did I ever breathe a sigh of relief. The dim glow of the few 100 watt bulbs were a welcome sight, like a sunrise after a dark and horrible night it was my sign I was saved from the dark abyss, at least for this month.

They say there were a total of five sub levels in that old factory and as far as everybody knew, I serviced them all. Between you and me, I couldn't tell you if there was even a forth, but if you're curious, we could go back there and find out together. I'll buy the hot dogs.

# Tuesday Morning Market- The Account I Couldn't Bear

I've worn a bunch of different hats over the years. Some were really fancy sounding and looked great on a business card. During meetings, I used to get looks from others who remembered me as *just a tech*; I can only guess what they were thinking. I am proud of those accomplishments, but out of all of the positions I held in my career, the most satisfying for me was being a tech, more specifically a commercial technician. I loved going to hospitals, factories, prisons, you name it. I saw so many different things. These were some of the most unique pest control experiences that I don't think you can get anywhere else. I was making pretty good money and I didn't have to make any calls to set my day as I did with my residential route. If there was a drawback it was that I was out the door at about 3 am every day but being a young man, this was just fine because my day would end about 1 pm.

Being a technician, however, is pretty demanding. Some of the places I treated on a weekly basis really wore me out. I would come into the branch office after my day to turn in my work and I'd sometimes see the salesmen just hanging out and care free. They were always in a good mood joking and laughing and flirting with the secretaries. Several of them were at one time technicians with whom I had worked and they were good guys. Now however, they wore ties and were always clean. It seemed they all were doing very well. They used to keep daily sales numbers on the board;

I'd look at it with amazement. It wasn't unusual for them to sell $1500.00 or more per day. I wondered how in the world they could do that when just a year ago they were running a route like me? Still, I was happy. My job had its perks too, but this subliminal promise of a better way was always in the back of my mind.

## Preparing For War

It was sort of a funny sight really, several managers from our region that I was so used to seeing in suits and ties suddenly donned green coveralls and caps as we gathered in a parking lot of one of the busiest food markets on the east coast. All the residential techs were there and even most of the sales guys showed up. But they weren't as giddy at 2 am as they were during the day. I never saw so many snap traps and B&G sprayers in one place. I felt as if we were going to war. We actually had planning meetings and strategized about this job like any combat team would. I'll admit, at least in the parking lot, we were pretty impressive.

This new sale was a huge open food market and it was the envy all of the branches in our region. Most of the vendors were only separated by half walls constructed with cinder blocks. The maintenance crew was just wrapping up with their mops and taking out the trash. Even though we were there they still turned off much of the lighting and it was as if every pest inside the place knew it was dinner time. Within minutes there were rats and roaches popping out from every crack, crevice, or hole big enough to house them. I think we all just stood there and gawked at the spectacle for at least 10 minutes. At this point it hadn't dawned on me yet but next Tuesday morning at 2 am- this would be my baby and I wouldn't have this huge crew that was with me now.

## Shock And Awe

Our strategy was to start the account off with the mother of all clean outs but I don't think any of us were prepared for the size of the building or the true population of the pests. Part of the plan was to paint Kill Master insecticide in key control points but we ran out about half way through. Our intent for the massive rodent population consisted of 'shock and awe' approach which we thought would wipe out the hoards in short order. We unpacked cases of snap traps and began setting them at every corner and junction a rat or mouse might possibly use. It wasn't even two minutes after we'd finish a zone and we began to hear the "snap" and "crack" of the powerful springs eliminating the first wave of unsuspecting rats. In the basement we doubled the amount of traps and we also applied tracking powder in suspected rat holes. In theory it was a pretty good plan and we actually bagged about 50 rats in our traps while we were there that night.

Most of the market was open space but we did have to wait for the maintenance crew to unlock the security gates of some of the larger stores that lined the outer walls. Standing there we witnessed german roaches crawling all over an electronic food scale that was still turned on. Now I don't know how much a roach weighs or how many in number were on that scale, but the stainless steel device was covered with them and the digital read out said it was about 3 and half ounces worth. What's worse, this place was downtown in the heart of my city route area. I had eaten here many times.

## The Solo Act

The next Tuesday came all too soon and I felt very alone as I pulled in the parking lot. I glanced around hoping I might see a friendly bug truck coming up the street but there was none. I felt like an ant in a shoe box as I entered the huge structure. The maintenance men were just finishing up and right on time the rats and roaches were coming out for their nightly feast. Our 'shock and awe' was more like 'sprits and hope' and it seemed to me like we hadn't killed a thing. Tuesday after Tuesday I showed up to the same nightmare. There didn't seem to be a service go by where a rat wouldn't jump up on my leg and use my body as a ramp to get to a counter top or ledge. Roaches boiled out of cracks in the hollow block walls and scurried about my feet as I flushed them out week after week. For what good it did I got very good and creative at rat trap placements. I would often find the lifeless carcasses in my traps hanging from pipes or rafters in the basement on the string I attached. Usually the rodents I caught were half eaten by their cannibalistic relatives and decomposing. The sanitation levels were so far below par and the sights and smells of rotting and contaminated foods made my stomach wretch. I began to dread this account and the herculean effort I had to put forth for little to no results. I only had until 7 am to get this massive job done each week but there wasn't enough time in the world to even put a dent in the pest populations of this account- not by myself anyway. By the time I left, I would be so worn out and I really grew to despise this job that had no end in sight and very little incentive for me. When the account was sold, it was the talk of the entire region because it was a prestigious place and a feather in our branches hat. For the salesman, I'm sure the commission was sweet, but for me at 15%, it only added up to about $20.00 per service, $5 bucks an hour. After a few months, I really hated life but especially Tuesdays.

## Time For A Change

The rest of my week was enjoyable as always but when 'market day' came around it was always an account I dreaded. The subliminal thoughts of becoming a salesman and more money with a clean uniform was becoming a dull roar inside my head. By this time, I was newly married and thoughts of my future and having more money naturally came along. Around this time there was an opening in the sales team and after about- 3 seconds of deliberation, I told my manager that I would like to have that job. I was kind of surprised at myself for stepping out like that. This was something I had never done before so it was a huge risk for me. He smiled as if he knew why. He lined up my replacement and asked me if I could take him on the route before switching positions in the company. My replacement's name was Jerry also and we had worked together many times on big bird jobs and apartments. He was (and probably still is) a great tech and a hard worker. He loved the route and caught right on but we hadn't had a market Tuesday yet.

When the day came to my surprise he did very well with it, or as well as could be expected. He was just as worn out and complained of the same things that got to me but he didn't share my absolute dread of facing this huge account. Perhaps he was still in a state of amazement of the commercial world and how different it was from the residential. My route at that time was really awe inspiring, never boring and truly a rewarding challenge that I looked forward to everyday. (except Tuesdays that is) As a commercial tech you got to use all the high tech tools that a residential guy would never even see. Your viewed as an important person in the branch and only the best techs are even asked to run the commercial routes. I often think back on my commercial route days. I think of all the great things I've seen and sometimes wish I never left. That is, until I think of Tuesday mornings and the market I just couldn't bear.

# Run of the Mill Pest Control

I was so very fortunate early in my career to have an account that taught me several aspects of pest control that some techs don't see for years, if ever. This one account taught me bird control, no baiting rodent service, grain fumigation, grain pest identification, dealing with government inspectors and proper communication, as well sanitation practices. Keep in mind I was still a residential service person, wet behind the ears when this account was shifted over to my route.

I remember pulling into the parking lot the first and only day I was to train with the guy who had been doing it. There before us was this huge old building that seemed to have 1000 windows and with it five or six even taller silos that stood like large castle towers. A river ran just behind the massive building and the banks were covered with large jagged rocks. My trainer for the day looked at me and said with a hint of sarcasm, *"You're gonna have fun with this one."*

The first thing I noticed was that this was a weekly account and I thought man they must have a lot of bugs. To my amazement when we unpacked our equipment for the job it didn't include my trusty sidekick B&G sprayer. Instead, we toted in two buckets. One filled with Avitrol bird bait (corn based bait for pigeons) and the other one was empty. By now I was confused, because up to this point the most commercial work I had done were some tiny delicatessens and an occasional office with a small warehouse but even then

I carried a sprayer and wore a tool belt. I couldn't even imagine how we'd do any kind of pest control for this huge facility with nothing but a couple of buckets.

Our first task was to check in with the operations supervisor and I'm sure he said something important, but I was in awe of this huge building and all the activity so I didn't hear him. Fork lifts were flying everywhere and conveyor belts moved endless streams of grain from one place to another, even up through a hole in the ceiling that was oh so high. There were hundreds of pallets stacked with thousands of bags filled with grain, all in a perfect row along every wall in painted aisles. Not a single pallet was out of line, not even an inch. We put our Avitrol bucket in a locked storage room and then both of us signed our names in a huge three-ring binder. I only caught a glimpse of the page but there were notes in columns and check marks in 'yes' or 'no' question boxes and some official looking red stamp in several spots on the page. I remember the supervisor looking at me, as if sizing me up. I could tell he had his doubts if I could handle the job. Right there at that moment, I had my doubts too.

## The Race Was On

We took our empty bucket and my trainer led me behind the first row of pallets where we found a 'ketch all' wind up rodent station surrounded by a bright orange steel frame anchored to the wall and floor. "*This keeps the ketch all's from being hit by a fork lift,*" he shouted over the loud roar of one such lift zooming by. "*Pick it up, look in the holes. If you got a mouse shake it to knock him out, put him in the bucket and keep moving. I'll do every other one.*" Right then as if a gun went off to start a race, he sprinted down the perfectly formed aisle. We were checking, shaking, dumping and winding the traps like two mad men. Each one had a number but he didn't tell me how many there were. I thought we'd never see the end even after we reached 100. All and all, if memory serves me, I think there were 143 traps, each one in it's perfect orange frame no more than 10 feet apart. I was surprised that we didn't really get that many mice and killing the ones that weren't dead already involved water; I'll just leave it at that. We ended up at the desk with the big book where we documented how many mice, which stations, moth or beetle sightings, and any sanitation recommendations. One of our nice orange frames did take a hit from a fork lift and we noted it in the book. You'd have thought the supervisor had just been told there was a bomb in the place and I think that thing was fixed before we ever left.

I thought maybe we were done with the mice or maybe it was just wishful thinking. We grabbed our bucket and all I was told was *"it's time to go up."* We went to a doorway where I fully expected to see a stair case but instead there was a large conveyor belt coming up from a hole in the floor and going through a hole in the ceiling. There were metal handles on the belt followed by thick metal plates. *"Grab a handle and step on a plate. Don't catch the bucket on the ceiling, or we'll have a mess!"* my tutor said as he rose through the ceiling and disappeared. Wow, this was so cool and worth the 1000 yard dash we just ran, so I latched on and up I went.

Much to my dismay, the ride ended on the second floor where we signed into another big book and ran yet another mouse-a-thon. This one wasn't so bad with maybe 90 stations. We also did the third floor which had even less. The fourth floor had none but we still needed to inspect it each and every week. It was much quieter with each floor we went up. My guide finally filled me in on what the entire job entailed as we walked around. My legs were a bit wobbly and I'm not sure I could carry that bucket of corn much longer. However, I was excited that we were taking that great conveyor belt in the sky up to the roof where I would begin to learn another valuable lesson in commercial pest control.

**Birds Eye View**

It's not every day that you get to ride a conveyor belt straight up through the ceiling with nothing but a small handle on which to cling and a tiny metal step not big enough for your entire foot but there I was going upward through the layers of this huge facility. Passing through each surface of this building was like a whole new world as I ascended upwards, but the employees didn't even look twice at this oddity of two men appearing from the floor and then disappearing through the ceiling. When I finally reached the top, my temporary instructor was already at the roof door waiting. With our buckets of bird bait in hand we stepped out into the biggest vista I think I have ever seen. Now I've been on many mountain tops and seen some beautiful views but something about the magic of riding straight up through the floors made me feel like an angel. Then, stepping out to the sight of tree tops as far as the eye could see with steeples sprinkled across the landscape gave me the feeling that I had just arrived at the Pearly Gates. I wanted to take a minute to drink it all in but my short term tutor had other ideas.

On the roof were several feeding stations that we were to make sure had plenty of the Avitrol bait for our pigeon control program. It was explained that only 1 in 29 kernels of this corn were actually treated with the chemical but that was more than enough. What happens is the Avitrol would make any unlucky bird that ate the treated kernel sick. Then the bird would take flight while growing sicker. The bird's 'distress call' would warn the other birds of the dangerous roof top and they would leave the area to look for another roosting site. It must have worked well that day, because we saw no evidence of any recent activity. He also showed me some areas that needed a product called Nixalite. These metal spines stuck up like a porcupines quills and were very sharp which prevented roosting on beams, ledges, or wherever you attached it to. I received a real quick crash course on bird control and found it simply fascinating. We made our way over to the silo tops via a covered walkway. We were able to get to all but one. *"You can jump to it if you're game,"* he said smirking, pointing to the three or four foot gap that led straight down to certain death. It was not much of a jump whatsoever but one slip and that would be it. Even though we could see pigeon droppings on the silo roof, since he said he had never done it, I also politely passed.

**More To Do**

It was time to head back down. Finally, this heavy bucket that I had to lug around was nearly empty which made my conveyor belt ride much easier. I thought we were finished for the day as we headed to the truck and I was thrilled with my new account. I've stated many times that pest control is a great job, because no two accounts are alike and there is always something new to see. However, my residential route at the time consisted mainly of row homes that were all alike. Quite often I'd do 10 or more on one street alone, so it could be so monotonous at times, cookie cutter pest control. This job would be the perfect adventure to spice up things and I looked forward to each and every service.

As it turned out there was more to do as we filled the empty buckets with snap traps and headed back towards this behemoth building which left me wondering just what we'd be getting into next.

Sometimes in the middle of a big job, you just don't realize how much energy you've expended until you get a tiny lull in the action. When you get that break, you wish more than anything you could sit for a minute and recoup a bit. I didn't have that luxury as we headed towards the bank of the river buckets in hand. Not wanting to show any signs of fatigue I kept right up with my trainer even if he never again would be with me on this account.

I'm not sure why, but aside from the Avitrol corn for pigeons there was to be NO rodent bait used at this facility, even outside. This made outdoor control a real challenge. I suppose someone (probably the salesman) decided at one time that the rats were coming from the river bank, so that is where the most of our efforts would be. To this day that really didn't make a lot of sense. Using only snap traps, we walked the banks looking for any rat evidence in the jagged rocks or burrows in the bank. We didn't find very much, even my instructor didn't seem too overly excited about this part of the service. "*Just put a few traps here and there, then we'll look around the back of the building,*" he told me trying to shout over the sound of the fast moving water. I never had any measurable success trapping this way but I did learn a valuable lesson. One of my traps was not hidden well enough and the following week I found that I had caught and killed a beautiful non target bird. Now, I grew up trapping and oddly enough, my first catch even then was a poor wood pecker who landed on my trap that was set for a fox. I'm not sure which time I felt worse, then or now. For all the mystique and excitement this job gave me in the first three hours, I wasn't sure I was going to like this aspect of the account.

## Not Quite Approved

Before leaving the facility we wrote in yet another big three-ring binder and checked in with the supervisor one last time. As with many managers and supervisors, these people are naturally skeptical and only feel comfortable when they're assured that the job at hand will be done correctly by the person doing it. This manager wasn't at that comfort level with me yet but he smiled and suggested we take a look at the basement so I'd have a full scope of the facility. He shook the hand of my mentor and he thanked him for his service. They both gave their quick assessments of me (which was kind of awkward), but both agreed that if I kept up so well on the first day I should be fine. I knew, however, that I had some major proving to do. Next week I would be on my own.

We did check out the lower level before leaving and it too was fascinating. There I saw where the process of milling the grain began before it ended up in the bags on the pallets in their own perfect rows. The grain was dumped from semi trucks into a huge screened hole on the parking lot level and piled up in huge mounds in an even bigger subterranean room. From there a very large stainless steel auger pulled the grain onto a conveyor belt and it disappeared into another room. We rarely did much on this level, except maybe chase a live rat around and try to whack it on the head with one of the few metal poles that were leaning against the walls. The poles were actually there for this purpose, inspector approved and numbered. Most often the employees took care of the rats in this area themselves but just in case there was a crafty one, I may need to know my way around. By today's standards this might seem barbaric but glue boards, baits, and traps were out due to the possibility of food contamination. Also, a lot of the rats actually tumbled out of the trucks with the tons of grain. So while they were a bit dazed, this was the quickest and most effective way to deal with the problem.

In another area of the lower level they did fumigations of the product for grain pests. This seemed really fascinating. I did sneak down from time to time later on just to see if I could watch them do it. The closest I got was a demonstration. I saw how they took long metal poles and poked them through a hole in the wall where the grain was stored. At the end of the poles, they would place fumigation tablets in a special cut out. Then by turning the pole when it reached the middle, the tablets were released and the fumigation began. I didn't know what these 'pills' were or just how toxic they are until years later. Fumitoxin is basically aluminum phosphide which releases deadly gas when exposed to air and moisture. Its main purpose is for grain pests but can also be used for burrowing rodents. The gas is highly mobile and there are strict restrictions on its application which is probably why I was never privy to any actual treatments.

The mill was always an account I looked forward to even though each week I performed the same task which is what I dreaded about my residential route. I learned quickly that the plant depended on me to spot wayward pests and to do my part in protecting millions of pounds of food. They actually listened to me if I spotted a sanitation problem building up, and unlike so many of my commercial accounts over the years, they took action based on what I recommended. I felt like a needed part of a team and a professional that soon everybody in the facility trusted. It wasn't that I had all the latest gadgets, because my tools were very limited. It was however, attention to small details that kept this highly scrutinized and inspected plant running smoothly with no major pest interruptions.

This is also exactly what I taught the rookie who took my place some years later. I remember I saw that same astonished look in his eyes that must have been in mine as well-that look of amazement and awe, *for this run of the mill account.*

# Stuck Under the Competition

I'm not fat by any means, and I used to say I could fit into almost any crawl space or attic there was. At least this used to be the case. Just a couple of years ago, this was put to the test. When I tell people this story I can't help but empathize with Forrest Gump. He'd tell his tales on that park bench and people were either fascinated or walked off in disbelief. I assure you this is true, but I'll understand if you raise an eyebrow.

Our office took a call from a management company that pretty much uses my company for anything pest related. This call concerned termites which was normal but the building they were in was anything but. This infestation was in a building that one of my fiercest competitors rented from this management company. Since it was them who reported the problem, it was fair to say that this particular competitor was not very happy to hear I was coming out to measure it up. Now I can understand that they wanted the job and why they might have been a bit miffed for not getting it. They did give a bid but their price was extremely high. Even if I wasn't the preferred vendor, I don't think they would have landed it. I can also see why they asked me to come out after five in the afternoon and park in the back. It was so I would not cause a stir with potential customers passing by on this very busy road. What I did not like was I was treated as if I were a spy sent in to tap their phones and steal their files. Their manager followed my every move and proceeded to grill me on every detail of what and how I would do the job. I don't mind when customers follow me so much, but getting the third degree is something of which I am definitely not fond of.

## A Complex Building

The building is probably 50 years old and had a few quirks to say the least. With a couple of doors to nowhere and the front wall of the structure was actually two brick walls about three feet apart with no access to the void in between except from the roof. This wasn't real obvious to spot and I needed to go back and forth quite a bit to figure it out. *My tour guide loved that!* Their sales room (where I did peek at a few sales figures-my bad) was a wooden addition built right on the soil, joists and all. The grilling, or should I say the "I'm smarter than you" tour, was not my best performance as I was taken aback with the complexity of the structure and the whole situation but I held my own. He was surprised I knew it was a crawl when I asked him where the entry was but unfazed he took me outside. We went behind yet another fake wall that concealed a boarded up door and the a/c units. I found a very small entry where the bricks had been busted out for some a/c lines and he mumbled gruffly, "that's the entry-that's the only way under". Well, there was no way I could fit in that hole and I certainly didn't see another entry, so now I really was in a dilemma of just how to treat this place if I couldn't get underneath.

## Mr. Happy

No more was I back to my office then I had a message from the management company. Apparently, I didn't make a great impression on my not so friendly competition and he let them know. I won't go into all that was said but the guy wasn't very nice. After five minutes on the phone, both the owner and I agreed the guy was nuts and he told me to schedule the job. The day was lined up but Mr. Happy Pants was having none of it. He said the work would have to be done on a Sunday so no one in town would know. Trying to keep my client happy, I agreed. From there the story just gets weirder.

Bright and early Sunday morning I was just about to start when Happy Pants showed up. He hardly said two words but I could just feel the joy in his heart. He looked at me, abruptly turned and went inside the office, I guess to catch up on some work. Yea, right!

To get under I had to try and make the hole bigger using my 'chipper tool'. To my dismay there were floor joists and pipes in the way and I couldn't make the hole much bigger at all. I'm not sure if I was delusional, to proud or just upset with this whole job but I decided to try and fit in this entry with the little extra room I created. I normally go head first but on this one I backed in and sort of felt my way with my feet. I got down to around my rib cage and it was getting very, very snug. Right about then Mr. Happy came around the corner, took one look and stormed off. I think he was mad because I was actually making my way in which I'm sure he was betting was impossible. About a minute later, I saw his vehicle pull away. For the first time I felt a little relieved, but that didn't last long.

**Helpless**

By this time I was almost in but my chest and arms couldn't configure no matter what I tried. I had a floor joists pinning me to the dirt, 50 year old pipes squeezing me like a boa constrictor and the bricks at the entry digging into my chest and back. I could tell that this was a losing effort, so I decided to climb out and see if I could somehow chip just a little bit more out of my way. That's when I realized, I was stuck. Wedged like a sardine in a can, I just couldn't move. Neither of my arms was free since I had contorted one underneath me and the other flailing helplessly pinned by the brick foundation. I tried digging my toes in to push myself forward but the loose sand gave way each time. I could feel my cell phone in my pocket but there was no way to get my hand to it. I'll admit I started to panic. At this point I would have given anything to see Happy Pants again. It seemed the more I struggled, the more panicked I became. After about 20 minutes, I finally just had to lay there and gather my thoughts. I decided to try and relax with deep breathing and let my body go as limp as possible. It worked. With a slight push from my foot and a forward nudge of my shoulder I moved just ever so slightly. I repeated the process many times and eventually my arm wriggled free. This was the leverage I needed and I was able to pull myself out.

I was worn out by the ordeal but so relieved to be free. I still needed to figure out how to get under this building so I went around the perimeter looking for any other way under and couldn't believe my eyes. There, on the opposite side of the structure was a cut out panel that was very well disguised. If I wasn't so desperate, I might never have seen it and for sure Mr. Happy wasn't ever gonna show me. When I unscrewed the panel it opened up into the crawl like a huge spacious cavern big enough for a bear. I was able to crawl around with ease and treat it just fine. The job actually was easier than I thought. The front wall and it's fake facade was reachable because of large vent holes and I could see the sky straight up where I thought I was gonna have to use rope and climb down. The brick foundation and what few piers there were had termite shields all the way around and the job wasn't nearly as challenging as I thought.

Before I left for the day I figured Happy would be calling, so I put a lovely note on a pier about 10 feet away from the entry hole he first showed me. I knew I'd need some solid proof that I treated underneath or this man would cry foul no matter what I said. You could see it from that small entry but it was far enough away that he couldn't say I just reached in and put it there. I buttoned up the secret passage and made it looked like I never used it. I really hoped that he would call but he never did. I renewed the account for two straight years until I got a call from the management company to tell me to cancel the contract. It seems each year Mr. Happy raised holy Cain when I came for the renewal and the management just couldn't take it anymore. They took over my contract but I doubt they ever went under the building. I hated to lose the money but I'll admit I was kind of glad to get rid of them too. I'll bet my note for Mr. Happy Pants is still sitting there on that pier unread. Still there to this day, stuck under the competition.

# A Wood Rotten Lady

Several years ago I was called out to do a wood destroying insect inspection for a real estate purchase. There was no realtor involved but I was to meet the prospective buyer at the home. Upon arrival I was met by a sweet elderly woman, and I could tell she was quite anxious about the home and its condition. She had already had the home inspector out who checked the roof, the a/c and everything they do. Now all that stood in the way of her and the keys to this quaint little home was me and my inspection results.

I'm used to people following me in my job and asking questions as I go but this lady did a little more than most. She pointed out almost every dimple in the wall paper and every scratch on the baseboard. Then she wanted a full explanation of why the damage wasn't from a termite or some other wood destroying bug. We went from room to room the same way. This small, two bedroom home seemed twice its size as the would-be owner practically pushed me to the side so she could take a closer look at every imperfection.

*"What could have caused that?" she'd ask in somewhat of a suspicious tone. Her look of disappointment and mistrust each time I told her it wasn't bug related was beginning unnerve me.*

## No Place to Hide

Now, normally crawling into a 120 degree attic is not something I relish but this time I was more than eager disappear into the darkness and crawl to the farthest end. Unfortunately, I couldn't stay up there forever. I could hear her calling into the darkness, asking for every detail as I slowly made my way out almost completely soaked from sweat. The hot summer heat and this lady were no less relenting as we went around the exterior of the home and I could feel fatigue setting in as we painstakingly checked the exterior walls.

Up to this point I could find nothing to report on the house but much to my dismay I still had to check the crawl space. I took a little bit of solace thinking that at least I could escape her probing eyes for a while. Perhaps it would be cooler underneath and my body might be able to recoup a bit. Just as in the attic, I headed for the farthest point but there was no escaping her calls from the distance. Making my way around, I came to a familiar trouble spot that most homes have. The floor boards and joists under the bathroom area were riddled with wood decaying fungi and my heart sank. In some states this would not be such an issue, but in Florida this goes on the inspection report and is considered just like termites. Part of me was glad to finally have found something for her but the other part knew this was going to set off a firestorm of questions.

## Where No lady Has Gone Before

When I came out, I told her of my discovery and as predicted she began spewing questions. She was incredulous to everything I said and almost came right out and called me a liar. I should have been angry or perhaps even taken aback. Instead, I simply repeated my findings and told her if she didn't believe what I told her, I had an extra crawl suit for her to go look for herself. Much to my surprise she took me up on the offer. Within a few minutes she was suited up, and we headed into a place that I never thought I'd ever see an 80 year old lady go.

When we reached the spot, I began to explain about the damage and what was needed to rectify the problem. To my astonishment, she said nothing at all. Instead she simply slid around towards the exit and crawled her way out. With my jaw dropped to the dirt floor, I watched this fiery ball of skepticism slither quickly away. I was speechless. When I finally made my way out, she was unsuited and getting into her mini van ready to pull away. Angrily she said she wasn't going to buy a damaged house and that was the last I saw of her. With my mind still numb from this strange experience I never gave her a receipt and to this day I've never been paid. I hope by now she's finally found a home that finally met all of her expectations. Somehow, I doubt she ever found a termite inspector that could.

# When Phobias Collide-The Professor And Me

What do you get when you cross a fear of chemicals, a 140 IQ, and a lady who practically screams bloody murder at the mere sight of a cockroach? Well, besides the makings of a great story I can share, it is perhaps one of the best examples of reason over hype I've ever had in my many years of pest control. It also gives me hope that the news of traditional pest control's demise has been greatly exaggerated.

## Back to School

For a college apartment complex this one is very small with only 14 buildings total, but it does have a little slice of everything that you'd find in the larger university settings.  Young adults from far and wide, learning to spread their wings, living together and getting first-hand experience and perhaps maybe just a bit too much pizza and way too much beer. The kids are great and not excessively unruly; they really can't be because a policeman, referred to as a 'courtesy officer' lives on the grounds. They even have an apartment set aside for the traveling professors. This one unit is nestled away in a corner and has always been the cleanest and quietest in the complex. Still it's 'connected' living, so what one apartment has pest wise is often shared with its neighbors.

I met the latest transient teacher while on a routine visit and she seemed nice enough. Well, once her look of horror went away as she gazed at my sprayer. "NO, NO, not my apartment," she shrieked as I explained my reason for being there. "I can't have chemicals where I live." Now she wasn't negative or condescending but she was definitely taken aback that pest control was now something she had to deal with. We agreed that I would skip her place for now but I was there if she ever needed me.

## The Calls Begin

It wasn't long after meeting her that my office took the call that this fine educator was seeing bugs. This time when I showed up I left my sprayer in the truck and only brought in some sticky traps knowing she wasn't ready for any kind of my brand of service. She literally let out a huge sigh of relief seeing me without *my arsenal of death*. I knew she was nervous about me coming but I really wasn't prepared for what I saw. EVERYTHING in her tiny apartment was covered in plastic or sheets with sticky notes attached. On each item were instructions and a history of exactly what she saw or was afraid of. *"That's a lot of work,"* I said with a smile, *"I'm sorry to disappoint you with just some glue traps."* I guess she sort of had a flash of embarrassment. She tried to play it off as if it were just a 15 minute project. She made no bones about being happy that I took this approach and complimented my sensitivity. She was also thrilled that I made enough time in my schedule to visit the four other apartments that surrounded her.

We sat for a while and talked about bugs of course but also the chemical approach in eradicating them. She was surprised about just how little chemical was in a finished mix, how long it would take for a roach to die while sitting in the dried solution and that I wasn't a big believer in fogging. Still, my short little chat couldn't sway her fears, so pushing through the plastic I placed a whole bunch of traps as we both hoped for the best.

Now the complex isn't infested mind you, and each summer we do a huge 'clean out' while the kids are gone. It doesn't take long in the school year however, for pizza boxes to build up and beer to overflow before pests take advantage. Our traps did do some good for the scholar but she couldn't even look at the bugs stuck in the glue. For all the dread she had over chemical applications, she had at least as much for insects. With each service, I spoke to her more about what would do her home the most good and I even started bringing my tools inside. My strategy of a surrounding barrier was fading and even though she was as clean as a whistle, the german roaches were starting to take hold.

## Enough is Enough

For such an intelligent lady she was tormented with fear but I could tell that the logical side of her brain was beginning to see the light. We didn't have 'organic products' back then per se or at least any that really worked (do we have those now?). For her, it was coming to decision time. She had to choose whether to live with a growing number of bugs on a daily basis that sent her into a tizzy, or have a professional service using chemicals of which she was deathly afraid. I'm not sure exactly what it was that I said or didn't say but there came a day when she had had enough.

We arranged for treatment on a Friday, because she was heading out of town. I met her at the door and she handed me the key. I began to explain (again) what I'd do but she simply smiled and said, "*I trust you.*" With that she left, and I was alone. There were no plastic sheets, no sticky-note instructions and for once, no lengthy conversations about the benefits of service. The only thing there was a card on the table (with kittens on it, I think) that said "Thank You" and inside was a crisp and clean $10.00 bill. This complex was a huge account for me back in the day and although I spent way more than 10 bucks on sticky traps, bait and time just for her, it was a symbol of victory to me. Of course, I took advantage of her being gone and treated as thoroughly as I knew how but I knew my barrier had to be invisible. I took great care in sinking all my products where they would never be seen. A few roaches scattered, mainly from the fridge but she had taken to heart my teaching on populations crashing with good sanitation by reducing moisture and even caulking up cracks. (She went a bit crazy with the caulk.) All in all this service was quick but I feared there would be dead bugs on the floor to greet my professor when she came home from her weekend jaunt and this would break the trust we built. Sometimes all the education in the world can't overcome the sight of creepy crawling bugs, dead or alive.

**The Breakthrough Takes Hold**

That Monday I didn't get any call from the professor, nor did I hear from her on Tuesday. Now I was a little worried. Did I kill her? Did she keel over at the sight of belly up roaches? I didn't see her for a few months actually but I knew she was there. I let myself in each month and did my regular maintenance service. There were no notes, no kittens on cards and no bugs thank God, but I could have used another $10 bucks.

When I finally saw her, the home was all boxed up and she was moving out. Her job kept her traveling, so it was off to another school. She told me that she did have some bugs to clean up but rarely saw a thing since I began treating her home. She was tempted to call but remembered my saying the residual would suffice if we just gave it time. It was like she was a totally different person. She was no longer held in fear by things so minute. *"You taught me a lot,"* she said, *"but I think I'll be living off campus in my next job."* We both laughed. I wished her well but I couldn't help but feel a little sad.

I wish I could say that my power of persuasion and vast knowledge of all things pest control changed this woman, giving her the will to overcome. I think, however, it came down to a choice of two perceived evils that turned into fears. One fear won out in the end and broke through the barriers and shed the most light. I guess this is what you get, *when phobias collide.*

# The Termite That Cried Wolf

As with any WDO (wood destroying organism) report, I make sure to list the things that hindered my inspection such as furniture, wall coverings, or insulation in the attic. The report itself states that it is a visual inspection only and there is no guarantee something isn't hidden deep in the wall where no one can see. That clause, put in by the state doesn't hold anyone back however, and almost 90% of all litigation comes from WDO inspections regardless of the legal disclaimers. Such was the track I found myself on with one such inspection.

### The Devils In The Drywall

I knew the new owners were quite picky, because they hounded me, the home inspector, and the previous owner for the tiniest details. They insisted on micro managing each phase of our work. Though I did a graph, typed up everything that I couldn't see through (which wasn't much since they made me move every stick of furniture), I knew that if anything were to go awry, this job would bite me directly in the butt. As Murphy's Law set in, two weeks after the inspection I got that dreaded call. My heart sank to the floor with the revelation that this home had swarmer termites.

Long story short, the swarm castle was sandwiched out of view behind some drywall next to the garage door and the exterior brick veneer. There was nothing visible at the time and very little even after the swarm, well that is if you discount the thousands of winged termites that filled the garage. The new home owner was livid of course and demanded to know how this could have happened. She seemed to settle down slightly as I reminded her that both her and her husband watched my every move and saw nothing amiss as well. For a while, it seemed that reason was the better part of valor but something changed for the worse over the next few weeks. Reason gave way to doubts, doubts to fear and then fears to out-right paranoia.

## Knowledge Is Power?

I'm pretty sure the new owner called every other company in town out for their opinions and estimates. I could just see visions of Judge Judy glaring at me, her glasses perched at the end of her nose as she passed down the stiffest sentence ever. I received many calls over the next few weeks. The lady kept referring to hidden damage and using facts and terms that normal housewives would never know. This 'new found' knowledge served no real purpose except to confirm this lady was being fed all sorts of tales. With no internet at the time my 'competitors' seem to take pleasure in fueling her already vivid and wild imagination.

No one in town had a dog at that time, or any kind of thermal device which might see into the walls to clue her in to the full extent of her problem. However, that didn't stop her from making the calls. Someone, somewhere down the line, suggested that she have a company cut the drywall away in several spots around the home where she was now convinced she had termites and thought there was the most extreme damage. They even went so far as to tell her to hand me the bill. She didn't like it much when I pointed out a WDO inspection is visual only and represents a 'snap shot' as to the condition of the home on that day and nothing further. I guess refusing to pay for her invasive inspection wasn't to her liking either.

## When Fear Turns to Anger

The paranoia this woman displayed had to be eating her up. She was genuinely distraught and besieged by things she wasn't even sure about, but I still felt bad for her. I had offered to treat for free and take care of any damage (if there was any) in the area the termites swarmed but I was sure my insurance company wasn't going to go for any exploratory surgery. I was dang sure I didn't have the money to foot the bill. With so many negative ideas put in her head, this lady became extremely angry when I refused to pay and called me everything but a child of God. She was convinced her newly bought home was riddled with termite damage and the dreaded word 'lawyer' was now being used on a regular basis. In these few weeks, she screamed at me, cried on my shoulder, joked, laughed, and even offered me dinner one late afternoon after another hour of scouring the empty home she refused to move into. All the while, I stayed calm and kept stating only the facts we knew. I implored her to not listen to those who were just interested in a sale and others who had no license.

In the end, wanting a resolution to this ordeal myself, I finally relented and agreed to have a contractor come in and cut away the walls. By this time I could feel the paranoia that consumed her, start to build in me.

## Wolf in Sheep's Clothing

The morning of this 'exploratory surgery' found me a nervous wreck. I saw first-hand how fear could grip someone even though I was quite sure that 95% of where the woman wanted cut away would be just fine. This was it, do or die- either I would be the goat and this woman's worst fears of termite damage were all true, or I'd be the vindicated one who was right all along. Either way I knew I was sick of this circus and wanted no part of a lawsuit. For me it would be the end of a miserable torture either way.

As the contractor's knife cut into original area of the swarm, the lady held onto her husband poised for the bad news and perhaps bracing herself for her worst semi self-imposed nightmare. He removed two large squares of drywall between adjacent studs. In an instant I knew I had dodged the biggest hit. It was what I had told her was most probable the entire time that was indeed true. The termites had constructed a large swarm castle with plenty of mud but very little damage. I had told her how swarmer termite wings were extremely fragile and snag and break in areas where feeding and termite damage occur. Therefore most swarm locations have the surfaces smoothed and groomed but there is literally no damage to the wood at all. For me I knew the worst was over but my schizophrenic client wasn't satisfied yet. As more walls were opened and nothing found, her insecurity slowly made way for some rational thought. Paranoia relinquished to fear, fear reduced to worry, and worry to doubt, until with the last opening it gave way to a sheepish admission, *"I guess you were right, Jerry. I'm sorry for all the trouble I put you through,"* she *whimpered.* Without missing a beat, I asked her to sign a statement that this matter was settled and closed and gave her the bill for the handy man that I had begrudgingly agreed to pay for.

You see I never gave in to her paranoid persuasions or the others who churned the waters of fear in her mind. While I desperately tried to tell her that she was being led astray I made the deal that I'd only agree to pay for her contractor if indeed we found termite damage. Fortunately, for me this time was a case, where the termite cried wolf.

# The Dousing

As a wayward spider dangled lifelessly from the ceiling at the end of its web, I could hear my homeowner from the living room shrieking and gasping in the most god awful way. By now, my ears were ringing and I had a headache having heard this same shrill alarm for the past hour and a half. *"There's another one!"* she exclaimed in her desperate voice. *"Come quick, spray him, KILL HIM!"* she commanded as her voice cracked. As I walked across the floor with the now hundreds of dead spiders and bugs crunching beneath my feet, I wondered just how I let this situation get so out of hand.

**Life's A Party**

This whole thing started from a simple call for spider control on a vacation lake home that was barely used. My would-be client seemed rational enough but she still let me know she was very afraid of these 8 legged monsters and wanted them gone. She was also leery of using pesticides but because she was having a party that weekend and didn't want the embarrassment of bugs and she thought I could sprits around for her to get rid of anything. My normally keen 'spidey sense' wasn't kicking in with what I now know was a bad day brewing. Even if it did, I was in no position to turn down a paying client at this point in my career. As it turned out, our schedules didn't mesh. So it wasn't until Friday, the day before the big shin dig that we could meet. This added an undue pressure to an already simmering situation.

The lawn crew was just leaving as she pulled in the drive. Smiling, she had a bounce to her step as she said hello to me and surveyed the freshly mowed landscape. I'm sure she had visions of a posh party as her envious friends frolicked on the dock of her beautiful lakeside estate. She didn't seem to have a care in the world and on the surface her vacation home looked great. I'm convinced she thought a quick service from me would be her final maintenance chore and she could go about the business of putting up streamers and balloons. This all changed when we could barely get to the front door .

## A Scene From A Movie

Wiping away the webs on and then opening the creaky front door revealed what years of neglect had left behind. The infestation of spiders with webs on every surface, all sorts of bugs and even a dead bird would rival any horror flick you've ever seen. It was dark and damp with the smell of mildew permeating this house of horrors. My client's knees wobbled as she gasped. She shrilled something inaudible and even welled up with tears and I'm sure her visions of a grand lake-front to-do went down in flames as her astonished eyes took in the spectacle.

It only took a few minutes of her brain processing this horrible situation before she must have decided she still had a chance to save her posh event. What I thought was a semi cautious woman had suddenly turned into the terminator from HELL! Oh don't get me wrong, she was still freaked out and could barely move but she managed to find a half way web free spot and began her 'shock and awe' campaign using me as her patriot missile.

I knew better than this alright but I couldn't even begin to withstand her screams and shrills every time a funnel or wolf spider came out of its protective cavity either running for cover or dying from the direct shot. *"EEEK, there it is. KILL IT!"* was her high pitched command. No amount of my even toned reassurance would calm her escalating fears and tone. Each arachnid that scurried or dangled from my attack just couldn't get 'dead enough'. Her persistence of more and more spray was very hard to dissuade.

## The Party Must Go On

After what seemed like forever and a day of being led by the nose from this irrational woman, I was finally able to convince her to head outside. She allowed me to clean up her infestation using a broom instead of the 'fogging machine' that my big mouth told her I had. *"You'll be locked out for hours if I fog. That'll put an end to any hopes of a party,"* I said in a baiting tone. This bit of information seemed to break through the otherwise hell bent demand for more and more chemicals. My broom was effective alright but it filled up with massive gobs of webbing in only a swipe or two. I used a tree trunk outside to scrape the sticky strands off as best I could and the mass of webs and writhing spiders that stuck to the bark was a spectacle in itself. So distraught the lady just watched in horror which by now I realized was due more to the fear of a flopped party and the embarrassment that would come along rather than of just the spiders themselves.

I spent all total three hours on this call and hardly a moment of it was in any ordered technique. I did manage to use several different products but when the same crack, crevice, or knot hole in the dark, dank wood was treated for the third time, for this client, it still wasn't enough. I found myself wishing I never answered the phone when she originally called. I really don't know if the party ever went off, but if it did, I'm sure of at least one woman who didn't enjoy it at all. She was probably nervous and stiff as she passed out hors d'oeuvres. Constantly glancing towards the toxic filled cavities and corners of the room, just sure that one hairy huge monster was waiting to pounce and ruin her façade that she obviously cared so much about. I'd bet she even went to the store and bought a case of Raid or room foggers and had her poor husband finish off what I would not. While I'm not a psychologist by any means, I'm sure there was more than one force at work on this woman. I'm sure she was afraid of the eight-legged freaks that took over her home away from home, but I believe she was even more aghast of the thought of her friends and peers seeing any deficiency in her otherwise ordered world. In any event, it wasn't the spiders so much as it was me, the technician, who was more the victim on this errant path - a path where phobias collide.

# Being Sued For Termite Damage

What does a fatal electric shock and a law suit against a termite company for a real estate inspection have in common? The answer - both are number one killers. Electric shock kills more technicians than any chemical ever has and real estate inspections are the number one reason for litigation against the termite company. Coincidentally, neither one involves chemicals that most fear cause deadly disease or contamination of property. Not to say this doesn't ever happen but if you listen to some people you'd swear the evil bug man causes untold death wherever his little truck takes him... but I digress.

Law suits are a scary thing and the system isn't really fair 100% of the time for either party. Facts are facts and truths are absolute, that is until you make it to that big ominous courtroom where decisions are not always made on the real facts or circumstance. I'm not a lawyer nor do I want you to take this story as legal advice. (Whoa, was that a disclaimer?) I merely want to tell you about my adventures in court, hoping that perhaps you can learn and avoid my mistakes.

**It's All In The Details**

My day in court was due to a WDO (wood destroying organism report) that I did on a vacant home, twice. The first report I did was for the bank as a repo home. Everything was fine. I crawled in the attic, checked the monolithic slab foundation, and all I could find were some old drill marks that indicated a previous termite treatment. The report was given and that was that. Three months later the home had a buyer. But since my letter was out of date, I was called to do another. Again, I went through the inspection and filed a report. I figured I was done. I did however, make one vital mistake that cost me dearly and hopefully you can avoid what I did not.

About two months later, a call came in that the new owner had flying termites and needed me right away. Now, I've handled plenty of these situations. I have done more than a few free treatments in an effort to make things right and once or twice, I've even paid for a door jam or other small repair. Most of the time this is even though I felt that these termites were not visible or detectable at the time of my visit. In this situation however, I immediately knew I could do nothing for the new owner. She was quite upset and nothing I said was getting through. She wanted way more than a few flying bugs and a two foot section of baseboard was worth. After a while (10 minutes) she told me to leave in no uncertain terms.

Now by all rights, I figured the law was on my side, the report states right on the front page that it is a visible inspection and only good for the day of the inspection. It also states that I am only allowed to probe or tap suspected areas but in no way remove or deface any of the property. The small board she ripped out did have evidence but it would have been impossible to see since it was just surface damage on the edge facing the wall. I also was a little suspicious since there were only five or six swarmer termites in a baggy and when she said that she went to Home Depot to have them identified, to be honest, I walked out of there just a bit cocky. I was most definitely put off by her ignorance but more so her arrogance.

## The Wheels Of Justice

I thought I heard the end of things when over a month went by, but one day while in the front yard, a sheriff came to my gate with a certified letter. I was being sued. At that point I lost all confidence and began to worry and second guess my every move. I called every friend in the business and got advice from anyone I could. The suit was for $3500.00 but at that time it might as well been a million dollars. I did think about hiring a lawyer and in retrospect I should have called one. The reason I didn't was because of a legal tip I got from a friend that I thought solved all my problems. *Piercing the Corporate Veil* was a term I had never heard before. My colleague told me since I was incorporated the lady could sue my small business but not me personally because of this rule. The paperwork listed me as the defendant and not my company- I was told I had no worries. I truly don't understand it all to this day but I thought between this and the plain language on the WDO form I would be fine. Not!

## Meeting In The Middle?

The first step to any suit is called mediation. This process puts the two parties in the same room with a trained mediator and they try to work out their differences, this is supposed to speed things up in a clogged system. My little 'Buzz Saw' however was still very indignant and refused to hear anything I had to say. She instead handed me a report from a repair company that wasn't licensed in termite control but 'specialized in termite repair.' This company's method of determining the extent of the damage was to drive an awl in the studs around the suspected areas looking for 'damaged' wood. If the awl goes in the wood, it is termite damaged, if it does not, then it is fine. Wow, what a scientific method! I asked her how he knew it wasn't wood rot or shoddy construction. That just made her angrier. By now, I was ready to scream and explained that I was in no way even allowed to do such a thing and how could she expect anyone to find the same 'alleged damage' using only their eyes? The mediator was useless in my mind as she didn't seem to comprehend what I was saying either. She seemed to be completely on my accusers side and just wanted me to settle. When I finally refused, we were done and the mediator scribbled some notes on a form and gave us each a copy. Then she sent us back out to the court room. When I looked at the notes and the boxes she checked, I think I had steam coming out of my ears. The note said I was not compliant and unwilling to mediate. But what it didn't say was that now I was more furious than ever and had had enough!

Back in the over-sized room and still feeling like I got railroaded in mediation, my accuser and I waited our turn to appear before the judge. While sitting there I took notice of all the different kinds of people in the courtroom and wondered about each one. Some were in suits and ties, some in work clothes while others had cut off t-shirts, tattoos, were unkempt and looked like they just rolled out of bed. What did all these people do to be here? I wondered how so many people could be in trouble? Are they criminals, rip offs, or worse? I couldn't help but feel like everyone was looking at me and thinking the same thing. I wanted nothing more than to get outside and get away. Calling our case, the judge barely looked up and mumbled a date as he dug through a mountain of papers. He told us to pick up our information at the clerk's office. Walking out, it suddenly dawned on me that what I hoped would be the end was just beginning, and I really wasn't looking forward to coming back.

## Consumed

The case was to be heard in about a month, during which time I got little to no sleep. I again made the rounds of calls and probably made a pest of myself to all who would listen. Everybody agreed with my side of course and encouraged me to stick to my guns. I contacted our state inspector who gladly forwarded me any information on the case he could but he avoided any extra comments like the plague. His advice was to pay the woman and run for the hills regardless of the facts. That really threw me for a loop. I thought about hiring a lawyer again and again. I even called a weekly talk radio show that featured two lawyers who answered questions. They too, were of little help and didn't wish to say anything concrete, so I made up my mind to go it alone and represent myself.

To prepare for the trial I gathered every bit of evidence I could find and even asked two current customers if they would come and speak on my behalf. The one who agreed was a client who had termites re-infest his home after a job I did. The termites destroyed a door jam and we worked it out to have his door fixed and upgrade his service to a baiting program in a way that was fair for both of us. My thought was to show the judge that I am not an unreasonable monster and my customer was happy to oblige. As part of the process, both my accuser and I were to send disclosure forms stating everything we would be bring as evidence including witnesses. Her list included the big box store employee who identified her baggy of bugs, the exterminator she finally hired to treat her home and the damage repair specialist. I knew I could blow the stock boy out of the water and I wasn't worried about the exterminator but the repair specialist was something of which I was unsure. I looked online and could find nothing about his technique of discovering damage. His yellow page advertisement boasted of termite repairs but offered up nothing on which to get an angle. Out of pure curiosity or paranoia, I decided to go by his address listed in the book. I don't know what I expected to find but the dump I pulled up to was surely not it. If this guy was any kind of specialist, he sure didn't reflect it in his choice of wash machine and old tires yard art.

Needless to say, the days dragged as this lawsuit consumed me far more than I ever thought it would. But when the day finally arrived, it seemed as if it was all too quick to come. Our time was set for late afternoon and I was surprised that we were called to a small conference office rather than the normal court room. My witness and his wife were dutifully there; my wife sat beside me. My heart had been pounding all day but as I looked across the table and saw the sloppy young termite 'salesman', my tormentor, and no one else- I suddenly grew a little more confident. I knew this kid knew next to nothing about termites and without her 'specialist' present, I figured the judge would not consider his malarkey anyway. According to my endless hours of research any testimony from a missing person would be considered here-say and therefore, not allowed. Did I tell you I was consumed? I even had the lingo down pat but this is not a profession I'd ever want to do. Besides I had my ace of 'piercing the corporate veil' and the WDO itself, which anyone can read says:

THIS REPORT IS MADE ON THE BASIS OF WHAT WAS VISIBLE AND READILY ACCESSIBLE AT THE TIME OF INSPECTION AND DOES NOT CONSTITUTE A GUARANTEE OF THE ABSENCE OF WOOD-DESTROYING ORGANISMS (WDOs) OR DAMAGE OR OTHER EVIDENCE UNLESS THIS REPORT SPECIFICALLY STATES HEREIN THE EXTENT OF SUCH GUARANTEE.

And the State of Florida's own web site states;

*"A "clear" report means that there was no evidence of wood destroying organisms infestation or damage visible and accessible to the inspector at the time of the inspection. It does NOT mean, however, that the buyer can be absolutely assured that there are no wood destroying organisms infesting the structure or that there is no damage from termites or other wood destroying organisms."*

So with all the momentum on my side (or so I thought), I was set. As far as I was concerned he could hammer down his gavel and call "case closed" for lack of evidence, but that shows how little I know. He didn't even have a gavel as he settled in to his huge leather chair, smiled and said, "I now bring this case to order."

**Have You Reached a Verdict?**

The sun was lowering in the sky; I could see it through the window. But that also meant looking just passed my accuser and I refused to let her think I was afraid to look her in the eyes. With my month long preparation, I became more and more convinced she was running a con game and was suing me for spending money, not termite damage at all. She is perhaps the most difficult woman with which I've ever had to deal with. Fresh from New York, she made getting a word in edge wise, at any time, a huge task. She was belligerent from the moment I met her and was actually the first person ever to 'kick' me out of a home. Our mediation was no different. Even the court appointed mediator could only chime in a time or two but still mostly just shook her head in agreement with this loon. Now, however, I knew I would get my say. This stately looking judge would have to listen to me and my eh-em, lovely indicter would be silenced.

I was a little unprepared for how the proceedings went. Not only did I have to present my own case but the judge told me I needed to cross examine my tormentor and her witnesses as well. (I thought he would.) I found myself stammering at first but since this whole scene played out in my head a million times over in the last month, it didn't take long for me to get up to speed. I put her back a bit by asking how many times she had walked through the home before buying it and others with her? She admitted that no one noticed anything abnormal and that she looked it over pretty carefully checking things like appliances and windows. "*Nothing amiss*?" I said starting to brim with confidence. She said, "*No*" and instead of a fiery retort, she was 'oh so nice and kind' like a southern bell. (what an actress)

When we got to the alleged swarm incident, I asked her what made her take the baseboard off the wall- why did she single out that one small board?. "*It looked okay and was solid, was it not?*" I asked. I could tell she was steaming underneath her new hair-do and bright cheery sun dress. She tried to say that the bugs came from there and it was eaten all the way through. At that point, the judge intervened and asked about the pictures she had submitted to evidence. I was waiting for that and I took each one she had and tore it apart with my well rehearsed rebuttal.

Without the board I couldn't physically show the magistrate exactly what I saw but I had a few pictures and notes on my copies of all of her pictures given to me in discovery. Most of her pictures were of 6×6 areas where her specialist had cut out the drywall exposing the hidden damage. My first point that we couldn't say for sure if it was her home since there was nothing else in the photo but drywall didn't go over so big. I did score however with a small white piece of paper that I explained, represented the drywall that was removed. I had cut it to just the right size and put it over each dark exposed area and asked her if she could see the damage behind the paper/drywall? She had to answer "*No*" and I was secretly thrilled with how things were going but tried to play it so cool. I added comments like, "*This is what I saw on my VISUAL inspection, do you expect me to see through walls?*" I explained the secret nature of termites, something she would never listen to before. I actually think she started to get it. My level of confidence grew and when I thought I had done enough I wrapped it up and folded my arms. Now it was her turn at me.

I obviously got to her. She rambled a bit and was getting nowhere when there was a tiny knock on the door. It was her store clerk witness who was running late. This shifted the focus to hearing what the corroborators had to say and I think she was happy with that. She wasn't happy with how both the judge and I tore him up. With no credentials besides breezing through the pest control aisle when a customer rang the call bell, it was easy to discredit him. Questions like how many wings does a swarmer have and what the difference is between that and an ant threw the stock boy. He had brought some books and began searching for the answer or some pictures. He was pretty much asked to leave at that point.

**The Darkening Skies**

Her other "expert" was a cocky sun of a gun; he was the young buck who finally sold her the extremely over price termite job which was listed in the damages I had to pay. While he could recall some talking points which I'm sure he got from his manager and some things he's heard in sales meetings, he really didn't help her out in my view. Something that I think resonated with the court however, is that he found many termite tubes on the slab. That threw me because there was not a thing on that house when I had checked it. It took several questions but like a greased pig I got him into a corner. He admitted that to find the subterranean evidence he had to physically dig to the footer. *"So nothing was visible when you walked around, no tubes? Live termites?"* I said as if I was Perry Mason who had my quarry trapped. *"No,"* he said knowing I had him. I continued, thinking I had to thwart his claim for the judge; *"On a WDO inspection are you mandated to dig with shovels, or is it a visual inspection?*" Hesitantly he said, "*Visual,*" but quickly added, "*if you suspect something you can.*" He was right about this but I couldn't imagine what he saw that warranted further investigation and his answer was the exposed termites inside. At that point, I felt like my point was made but I might be on thin ice. I shook my head to the judge indicating I was through. The time for the verdict was growing near.

By now the sky was dark; it felt like we had been in this room for ever. It was the judge's time to talk and he asked me many questions about my qualifications, training and experience. I knew for sure I had been effective and all that my accuser could do was keep referring to the damage they exposed and say that I had missed it. To my surprise, she did bring up her 'repair specialist' when he began asking her some questions. She showed the judge a letter he typed and sent her knowing he wouldn't be there. That wasn't in the disclosure. I thought for sure he'd toss it out just like the store clerk, but instead he seemed intrigued. Suddenly, I didn't feel so confident and I could feel my victory slipping away. Politely I waited for him to address me one more time. It was now or never for my ace card of 'piercing the corporate veil,' and right then, as if on cue, he brought it up and explained in legal jargon that he knew all about my protections under this veil but he was not going to recognize it and had every right to do so. Again, it was legal speak, and dumfounded I said nothing at all. He also explained that had I not made one specific mistake, he would think differently about this case. Horrified, I awaited my fate.

## The Gavel Drops

If you'll remember, I mentioned I did this inspection 'twice.' The first time was never in question. I listed the termite drill holes as previous evidence of a subterranean termite treatment and all the standard things. My second report however, was missing one little check mark. It was a small error on my part but I hardly thought it would make the difference. I almost always compare old WDO reports when I know I've been to that address before. That way I can check to see what's changed and just make sure I didn't miss anything- this was one time I did not and I failed to list evidence of previous treatment. The judge explained that not disclosing information about a previous treatment to the client meant she had no chance to investigate further the possibility of termites or damage. For that, he found I did not live up to the job for which I was hired. Further, he said that even though her witness was not there, the damage was undeniable and I would need to foot the bill for repairs.

I was a bit flabbergasted with his allowances and of these last minute decisions but I realized the one truth he said that put this whole thing squarely on me. My job is to give a client, tormentor or not, all the information. In doing this, the ball is in their court (pun intended) and they at least have the opportunity to use it to make a more informed choice. Although I was still in a daze with the days proceedings I did feel like a huge weight was lifted off my chest. Vindication or not, I could now finally move on with my life.

With the final verdict in I gathered up my papers, thanked the judge and my wife & I made our way out. Up ahead we saw that my client and her witness were gleefully already chatting up the big victory. We purposely walked slowly enough for them to get in the elevator and have the doors shut before we got any further. Oddly enough, I felt so much better that this was over. I knew I had learned a lesson I'd never forget- my torment was gone. The plaintiff did have to call later that week to arrange how she wanted to receive payment but to our surprise she was civil and polite. I've not heard or seen her since but that period in my life is one I'll never forget. By law I have to keep records in storage of all my WDO's for seven years before I can discard them. Even though it has been over to 20 years now, this report has a special box and still sits there today. The words I wrote on the box are faded somewhat and silverfish have eaten away some of the lettering, but you can still see the only remnants of this faded part of my past, "CASE CLOSED".

# Rafter Tag And Bird Control

I grew up in the good ol' state of Iowa. We always lived in very old farm houses with barns, corn cribs and abandoned tractors in the yard. Now we weren't farmers per se, we just rented the home but we always had a horse or two around as well as other assorted critters. Since the Wii wasn't invented yet, we had to get a little creative to have fun. Rafter tag was an all-time favorite which we would play for hours on end or until one of us was bleeding or half unconscious on the ground. The game was just like 'tag', but with a little twist. Our game was played in the rafters of the old rickety barn and NOT touching the ground was the only rule. As you can imagine, this made for some dangerous play time and we took some real chances all in the name of not being 'it'. I guess this prepared me for my career in pest control, because I have definitely had to pull a few olympic type moves in some of the work I've done. This is especially true of bird control which I'm not sure I could've done except for my endless hours of training- playing rafter tag.

**The Sail Cloth Factory**

One huge job I sold was an old sail cloth factory converted to apartments in downtown Baltimore. It was a cool building because they kept all of the old beams and machinery. Each apartment was completely unique. In the middle of the building was a huge atrium. The wood expanses crisscrossed like a magnificent cathedral fit for a king. The problem was that the pigeons loved the handy work as well and they were making a mess. Since I sold the job I guess it was up to me, or perhaps maybe no one else was crazy enough to do the work, but the pigeons had to go. Since I worked for the world's biggest pest control company our safety equipment gave us no trouble at all. *Oh, that's right we didn't have any!* So there I was with a caulking gun of 'roost no more' and three spare tubes facing these enormous beams that vaulted into the sky. Even the pigeons were cooing in an uneasy way as I began to shimmy up the wood that probably hadn't been touched by human hands in over 80 years.

The massive beams that looked so big on the ground were now suddenly slim and slippery from dust and uh, poo. My plan was to crawl a little, reach behind me to squeeze out the goo and work my way up the beam. I hadn't considered how draining this would be and my muscles were soon giving out. I had my spare tubes tucked in my shirt against my chest which really was uncomfortable, and to move I had to holster the gun in my pants down the small of my back. I think you can guess where the pointy tip went. Ugh! It seemed like it took forever to get to the top and I was becoming more and more drained. When I made it I thought I might never make it down. I was oh so high and unlike rafter tag there was no escape route or rope swing to rescue me this time.

**No Rest For The Weary**

I was able to rest a little at the peak and actually sit up. But that was a reminder of where some of the 'roost no more' had dripped and I was beginning to painfully understand just why the pigeons hated the stuff.

Changing my empty tube, I decided not to carry it any further, so I dropped it down to the courtyard below. I have never seen anything take so long to hit the ground and that's when I realized just how high I was. *(Well, there was that time my brother fell off the corn crib wall in one of our tag games. That too was slow motion as he belly flopped to the ground- danged if that was the only building on the farm with a cement floor. He of course blamed me but I was cleared of all charges. But I digress.)*

The next beam was easier, because I was going down and it really took no energy at all. Other than needing a cold rag on my cheeks, it was so easy sliding down and treating the old rafter and within minutes, I was safe on a catwalk.

I was so happy to be on solid footing, I was surprised at how my legs were shaking and how numb my arms were. Looking up, I saw that my treatment had worked, because not one bird was walking on the two beams I had treated. For a moment, I felt a real sense of accomplishment. That went away quickly however, when I made my way to the next set of these rafters from hell and thought, *"Only four more to go and I'M STILL IT!"*

# Two Tech's And Their Peak Performance

Bird control means one thing, going where the birds are and that sometimes can be very dangerous. Leaning out over roof tops, walking on thin ledges and hanging from the last rung of a ladder used to be pretty common place when it came to servicing bird control accounts. Today, thank God, we as an industry have a little more sense and use equipment like cherry pickers, scaffolding, safety harnesses and of course, the old trusty ladder. They say anywhere from one million to one BILLION birds die every year by striking buildings (mostly windows) but thankfully there are not too many serious injuries (at least reported) of pest control technicians doing bird work. While I'm not surprised at this for today's bird control workers, I am amazed that I didn't die back in the day when bird work was a huge part of my route. You may remember my story of the flour mill and how I refused to make a very dangerous jump just so I could treat a silo for birds. That was one sane moment in my career but there were a couple of other times when sanity had 'left the building'. (Yes, pun intended.) This is one of those.

### Foolish Decisions And Lack Of Safety

Baltimore was riddled with pigeons and when they decided to roost somewhere it got messy very quickly. I was a newer salesman when I was called out to a residential home for just such a reason and was surprised to see just how many of these 'r*ats with wings'* could fit on a roof's peak. This was an older styled home and the pitch on the roof was very steep with slate tile shingles that were very slick. The home owner was desperate for relief and I, being young and foolish was ready for the task. There was no place to put any Avitrol bait stations which would have been the easiest way to do the job. All I could figure to do was attach Nixalite strips from one end of the peak to the other. Since the job was sold at such a high price (all bird work was), our commercial tech was assigned to the task. I had worked with him many times on all sorts of jobs. His name was Jerry too and he's the one who took my old position as the commercial tech. As it turns out, Jerry had more sense than I and thus wanted none of this job. You see, working for *THE WORLD'S GIANT* in pest control we had a lot of advantages. All the resources were available with just one (or 100 calls), but safety equipment wasn't ever tops on their list that I remember. We had no ropes, no harnesses and nothing more than an extension ladder that *almost* got us to the top of this roof. Since the job required two of us-one to hold the sharp strips and the other to glue them down, I had to have his help. After about an hour of coaxing, we finally made our way up the ladder.

I had to be right behind Jerry prodding him along inch by inch or he wasn't gonna move. I carried the glue gun and the Nixalite strips which are extremely sharp. Coaxing him along, the strips kept poking me as if I were carrying an angry Porcupine. It was a windy fall day and when we reached the peak we were both struck by how high we actually were. We had to straddle the peak and inch forward by sliding across these roof tiles that provided zero grip. The now more powerful wind was blowing directly in our faces. Jerry did not want to move and was getting more and more apprehensive by the minute. Now I'm not exactly afraid of heights and I didn't have much of a problem being up there, but with no room to trade spots I had to get him going. The plan was to scoot across to the other end and work our way backwards. I knew if we could just get to it, Jerry's mind would at least ease up just enough and he would concentrate on the task. Plus, I couldn't carry enough strips in one haul, so navigating up and down on the precariously placed ladder for more supplies was something he would not want to do.

## A Plumbers Perspective?

Sure enough, I finally persuaded him to get moving but just about each time he pulled himself forward a big gust of wind would come by. Poor Jerry was really having a hard time. I know it sounds mean but I couldn't help but laugh. You see Jerry was no small guy. Well, I mean he was a little on the hefty side let's say, and by this point he was bent over just hugging that ridge with all his might. He wouldn't sit upright to save his life and I think some of those slate tiles still have his fingernail marks in them to this day. In this awkward position his shirt became untucked and his, eh, derriere started to show for the entire world to see. (well just me and the pigeons anyway) With each inch forward, his plumbers profile shined a little more and I couldn't help myself.- it just got me cracking up. Ol Jerry didn't like me laughing for sure and he swore he was gonna kill me if we ever made it down alive. I couldn't tell him why I was amused because that might have given him the final reason to quit- Lord knows he was looking for one.

## All The worlds A Stage

When we at last reached the other end of the roof Jerry had to sit up but that didn't help matters at all. The home was on a hill and the ground below on the front half was so much farther down than it was on the back side. This scared him even more than he was already but we both knew, the only way off this roof was to get the job done. Jerry began working at slow but steady pace.

Going backwards was much easier for Jerry but boy did he whine when I had to go down for more strips. I could hear him yelling for me to hurry as I smiled to the now gathered crowd of interested neighbors all gawking upward at this two man spectacle. When I reached the top, he was back to hugging those slates. His exposed derriere was red from the whipping wind but by now I felt more sorry for him than I did like laughing. At one point he dropped the glue gun and his body jolted as he scrambled for the only safe position he knew. I think he poked himself pretty good on the Nixalite but his frozen vocal chords never made a sound. I thought I would never get him to move after that and actually thought I'd have to call the fire department. We did however, manage to finish the job and the small group of onlookers actually clapped when we finally touched ground. Poor Jerry was just shaking and I tried to pass it off as a routine job but I was back to giggling which I'm sure Jer didn't like one single bit. When his nerves finally calmed down enough, he muttered a few things I can't repeat here, headed for his truck and sped away.

The job was done and I cleaned up, got paid, and headed out for my next call. I didn't have the heart to tell Jerry that this job needed to be checked monthly to fulfill our one year contract. I thought I might save that for another day. I can only hope if Jerry ever thinks back about that job he can chuckle like I still do to this day. The day two techs reached their peak.

# Two Rats, A Spear And Just Who Got Stuck

It was a dreary fall day in the city. As usual I was chasing down leads looking for anyone who'd say yes to my proposal of pest control service. I've always been a better technician than salesman so with cooler weather around the corner, fewer bugs would be out and I'd have to take anything I could get. But the colder days meant rodent activity would be gearing up. Although it wasn't like the panic that hit the streets in the springtime with swarming termites, it was at least a little action and people would still pay good money to rid their home of mice and rats.

For a pest control salesman, having a great technician in your area was like solid gold. My guy was just that. My route tech's name was Tim and he and I worked very well together. He was a very able tech, great with clients and knew a great deal about a lot of different pests and how to treat them. What I liked best about Tim however, was that he never said, *"No!"* to any of my hair brain and border line dangerous sales. He'd climb a tree to sprits a bee's nest or even prop a ladder on the roof of his truck if his standard six foot ladder wasn't high enough. The guy just did what it took to get the job done and always had a smile on his face which my people loved. That's why it didn't surprise me that Tim's tool box on his truck resembled a cache collection of really wild looking weapons. Some of Tim's tools just didn't seem to fit the mold of pest control but he swore they all had a legitimate use. There were mid-evil looking traps and ninja styled throwing stars, knives, clubs, snares and even a 10 foot long spear complete with the decorative little tassel near the deadly sharp head. I used to help him on much of the work I sold but never once saw him use any of his deadly arsenal. I often teased him about the stuff but he just smiled and said, *"One day you're gonna need one of these, then you'll be glad I have it."*

## Rush Hour

In those days, we didn't have cell phones but beepers were pretty efficient and sped up service quite a bit. Companies actually bragged in advertising about this technological advantage as an added reason for hiring them. Ours was one of those companies. I felt the buzzing on my belt as I was making my way through the mid-morning traffic on I-695, Baltimore's version of the Daytona 500. I figured I'd wrestle with the holster once I got to my exit so I could keep my hands on the wheel in this jungle of fast moving cars. By the time I got the fifth vibrating alert in a row I figured it was either a great day for leads or a real emergency. I pulled off a few exits ahead of schedule. The message was to call the office for an urgent service that CANNOT WAIT, so I found the first phone booth I could and plunked in my 35 cents. It was a rat job in Pikesville (just outside of the city). They had already alerted Tim about the job and he was told to drop everything and meet me there. Now, I have been called to rat jobs a hundred times by this point in my career, but never was such urgency placed on immediate response, so I asked why. The rush turned out to be that this rat had wandered into and was now trapped in a little old lady's kitchen and she was scared to death. The office told me that the job was already sold for $125.00 but it had to be done NOW or she was calling someone else. Although I didn't contract this job and I thought the price was a little low, I was told I would get commission regardless. So off I went to bag a guaranteed sale, a rat and a few extra bucks.

On the way over, I remember wondering how I was ever going to get a live rat out of a home. In my job, I see the droppings and evidence left behind but rarely do I see the live rat face to face. Normally, I set some bait stations or a few traps, leave and just wait for the rodent to come out that night. The next day I look like the hero when the lifeless body of the rodent dangles from my trap and the client is relieved feeling they got their money's worth. On this job, the dang thing was in plain sight and apparently chased the lady as she barely escaped with the phone to call us. I thought maybe I'd open all the doors and chase him out, or set 100 snap traps surrounding the kitchen. Maybe she had a gun I could borrow? In the end, I had more questions than answers. As I pulled up to the house however, I had no such trap for what else I would come face to face with.

### An 80 Year Buzz Saw

The 'sweet helpless little old lady' was waiting for me on the front porch but like a buzz saw, she immediately tore into me with demands and questions. She caught me by surprise and wanted to know everything I was going to do about this problem. If what I said didn't line up with what the office told her, she really flipped her lid. I felt like I was being attacked even though I'm the one who dropped everything to help her. All this time I was being interrogated I was thinking about this rat that could be escaping- if that happened, I knew I'd never hear the end of it. Just then, like a godsend, Tim, my trusted technician came walking around the corner. He stated in a very loud take charge way, "*I parked in the alley to be near the back door. Let's bag this thing!*" He must have heard the barrage with which I was being hit, and smooth as silk, he took command of the situation.

Row homes in Baltimore were pretty much all the same, back doors were from the kitchen and led to the alleys which is where rats and mice loved to run. Tim figured right away that this thing snuck in an open door and then got trapped inside. He told me to go through the front and he'd have a surprise waiting for me round back. I was really nervous finding a swinging door that separated the living room and kitchen. With no handle I was forced to push the door open but couldn't pull the door shut if I had to. Was the rat right there waiting to pounce? Should I go through slowly and risk it escaping with its blazing speed, or pop through quickly and surprise it? Either way I couldn't effectively control the swing of the door and I was at a disadvantage. I decided to go slowly.

**Face To Face**

As I pushed the door open, nothing caught my eye right away. The kitchen was clean and orderly with nothing out of place. Tim was standing at the back door facing the alley and I could hear the little old lady now peppering him with her endless questions and comments. "*What's he doing in there? Your office said you'd get rid of this thing! When you gonna put some traps out*?" Tim never flinched. Somewhat relieved because I had not seen anything face to face in this small but very bright and light colored kitchen, I took a few quick steps towards the back door. Just then a movement caught my eye and I froze with my hand on the knob.

There in the corner behind the only dark appliance in the kitchen (a coffee maker), was a pretty good sized Norway rat. Both of us stood motionless hoping neither one of us saw anything even though our eyes were fixated on each other. It took a few minutes but the rat sort of settled back in the shadow of the brewer. I felt I could now open the door and to Tim's credit he hadn't moved a muscle and was still saying, "*Yes ma-am, and no ma-am*" to this very belligerent seasoned citizen. Even though he wasn't treating anything, he was still just as important by running interference with my would-be attacker leaving me free to do the job. Opening the door revealed another key reason Tim hadn't moved or turned to look inside. He was hiding a very deadly a spear behind his back. He wiggled his hand back and forth so as to signal me to grab it and I did so without our client seeing a thing. I took the weapon and closed the door and found that this spear actually unfolded to a 10 foot long instrument of death. I don't know why I didn't insist on some snap traps or even just leaving the door open. I could've chase the rat until he ran into one of the traps or just let the thing out the back door. But, the spear was in my hand and like an ancient warrior going up against a loathsome beast, I poised my weapon and prepared to strike.

Jerry Schappert

## Getting Stuck

By now Tim was turned around and had his face pressed against the window wanting to see the carnage. This infuriated our elderly tormentor but she relented when in an authoritative tone he barked out *"we're just about to take down this huge hairy beast and I can't be responsible if you get in the way!"*

The spear was so long I had to stand in the opposite corner and I had only a foot or so of room to maneuver. My heart was pounding in my throat and my hands were shaking as I put the lethal shank within six inches of this greasy rat with beady eyes. Almost as if he could feel the tension through the end of the spear, the rat shifted to the other side of the coffee maker. All the while Tim was peering in giving out instructions, his voice muffled through the glass. I was sweating bullets, face to face with a rodent, armed only with an ancient spear that was longer than the room. To match his move I had to pull back my weapon to avoid the coffee pot and stay under the cabinets above. I quickly and smoothly tried to line up for another try. The rat wanted none of it. With my quick jolt he bolted towards the end of the counter and most likely his escape when suddenly Tim banged hard on the door. This paralyzed the rat into a moment of confusion and that was all I needed to drive my ancient tool of warfare into its slimy greasy body with a bone crushing thud.

It took a minute for things to settle in for me but Tim was all excited about the kill. He jumped around like a boy on Christmas day who just got a Daisy BB gun (every boy's dream) and even the unhappy homeowner took a step back and was quiet. I folded the spear up a bit just so I could get out the back door. The impaled rat was lifeless on the spear's point as I emerged from the back door victorious. The old lady looked shocked and there were even a couple onlookers from across the alley who heard the commotion. They all gasped as I held up my kill like a proud hunter's trophy. Tim was delighted to say the least that one of his ghoulish pest control tools actually came in handy. I think he went a bit overboard with our client, almost taunting her on how we got the job done. Probably not wise.

While most people would have been extremely thankful that not only did we come out the same day they called, but also that we actually killed the rat and removed it from their property so they'd have no more worries. Our little tornado didn't see things quite this way at all and suddenly ratcheted up the tone and verbal attacks. She claimed that since we promised traps, baits, glue boards and a return service that she was NOT GOING TO PAY for what she didn't get. Both Tim and I were flabbergasted. Even though we had the dead rat on the end of the spear we could not convince her she got her money's worth. We weren't allowed back inside so we could use the phone to get help from the office so Tim and I decided to leave. We figured our manager would straighten things out and everyone would eventually get paid, after all, we really did stick it to that rat. The story went 'viral' (by beeper I guess) throughout the company and we were considered legends for a time. That was all fine and dandy until the next commissions' checks came out and our little pittance for this heroic deed was never included. I guess in the end we were really dealing with two rats in this ordeal, and the furry little one wasn't the only one who got stuck.

# My Broken Ankle, My Unbreakable Wife, and My Fragile Business

Struggling to start a new business is tough in any economic climate. Do it when times are bad and the competition is out there clawing and climbing all over you just to get that all important client before you do. When things are good, hesitant entrepreneurs suddenly lose their shyness and companies are coming out of the wood work. Then the fight for new customers is just as fierce but the punches just come from different directions. Needles to say, starting a business, any business, is very difficult. If you add unnecessary or unforeseen problems, it can be and so often is the nail in the coffin. Such was my dilemma, twice early in my career.

For those of you who don't know me, I'm a 100% kind of guy in almost any endeavor I'm in. I play in 24 hour paintball tournaments, volleyball, mountain bike, crawl under and all throughout houses for a living and even teach Chuck Norris karate. (OK that's a lie, but I guess you get my point) The thing is when I do these things, I play hard and I play to win. Now that's great when you're a teenager and feeling immortal but hardly the recipe for good things to happen when you're in a brand new state, don't know anyone and you've started a new business. Such was my dilemma in my early days and except for the grace of God and my unselfish wife, I made it through despite myself.

## Side Out

Like I said, I'm into sports, and one volleyball season I was crashing around, diving off the walls for digs etc., when I had an intimate encounter with a trash can. If you've ever seen the pictures of Brett Favres purple leg after the 2009 NFC Championship game then you have an idea of what my leg looked like after that dumb move. I had broken my ankle and pretty much ruined myself for making any money for my family since I was just a one man bug company at the time. To make matters worse my little bug truck was a stick shift and there was no way I could drive that thing let alone walk. At that time, my route was pretty small but I had enough to keep me busy and somehow still pay the bills. Taking time off was never an option but crutches and a clutch were not going to work either. Not to fear, come Monday morning, my wife, a registered nurse quietly put on a Bug Doctor shirt and simply said, *"Let's go."* For the next week she braved the brutal Florida sun and did her best to treat the houses, spray the yards, and put up with me and my whining. For the most part, the customers got a kick out of it. Some that are still with us to this day tease and say, *"When you gonna send that good looking tech back out?"*

## Sneak Attack

A year later, maybe less, my self destruct mode kicked in again but this time on the battlefield filled with paintballs. I was sneaking in the enemy base, crouched over so as not to be seen when suddenly my back went out like nothing I had ever experienced before. My body crumpled to the ground and I was powerless to even move. I wouldn't wish that torture on my worst enemy and I feel sorry for anyone who has felt that same level of pain. This happened on the weekend but it was obvious on Monday morning, I wasn't going to be able to exterminate a thing.

I was unable to move and in tremendous agony even when I slept. There was no way I could even bend over to tie my shoe let alone treat a home. Once again, my selfless bride donned the shirt that I had promised she'd never have to wear again and got out there in the trenches. By this time I had some pretty decent accounts but they weren't easy. As she drove from stop to stop, even the slightest bump in the road sent excruciating pain throughout my body. I couldn't even get out of my truck so I had to tell her what to do at each job and she went off alone, doing what I at times can't teach techs with years of experience to do. Sometimes she'd come out 4 or 5 times to get instructions but she never complained and her service turned out to be very effective.

I eventually got through this painful ordeal, at least enough to work by myself. I had chiropractors, electric therapy, injections, the whole works. Even when I could get around, there were times I couldn't even bend over to tie my shoe. I was nagged with back pain for 10 years from this one episode. It wasn't until a client insisted I try her inversion table that I finally found relief.

The point of my story is that start-up pest control companies are very hard to get up off the ground, and that's even if everything bounces your way. Many new firms start every year in this town and it isn't until sometime later that one realizes many of these businesses have just quietly slipped away. Now if you like skydiving, mountain biking, or anything that could quickly incapacitate you, my advice is to at least have a back up plan. But as your lying in bed trying to recuperate, don't even think about calling my wife. She's retired and has hung up her bug shirt for the very last time. Thanks Honey!

# Crazy Bee Work I've Done

Most sane people approach bee or wasp extermination with protective suits, the right training, equipment, or even go out at night to lessen the chance of getting stung. That didn't seem to dawn on my employers at several places I worked early in my career. Armed with only a puff duster and a can of aerosol, I was sent into many a hellacious job. It's a wonder that I survived at all. Here are a couple of quick stories of bad stinging pest work that could have turned out oh, so wrong.

## Scaling To New Heights

On my route in Baltimore I was called out to a second story apartment that had a bee's nest in a couch which was on a deck over-looking the parking lot. This was $175 dollar job but to my dismay, the tenants were not home and there was no way to get in. I had planned to do my dirty work with the protection of the sliding glass door if things got hairy, but now I had to come up with plan B. The pillars holding up the decks were made of fancy designer bricks and looked easy to climb, so I put my duster in my mouth like a pirate would his knife as he boarded an enemy ship and headed up. I really didn't have any intention of treating the nest because company policy was to always get paid for bee work at the time of the job. That and scaling a two story wall wasn't going to endear me with my office but at least I figured I could see what I was getting myself into.

I could hear a steady buzzing and there were a few bees going in and out of a hole in the back of the couch but I've seen worse. As I surveyed the situation, I thought the nest must be small since there wasn't a steady stream of incoming and outgoing workers. I decided to *puff* a little of my dust of death *ever so slightly* into the hole. Big mistake! Within seconds the air was filled with angry dive bombers. As I fell back against the wall my hand clenched and I'm not sure that was by instinct or divine intervention. Either or, I believe it saved me from great harm.

**Divine Intervention**

This inadvertent squeezing of my duster sent a huge plume of dust into the air and all around my head. I distinctly remember seeing bees come through the cloud almost right to my face. It was as if they were coming in from out of focus into a full sharp view. Oddly enough, they turned and flew out of the cloud as if they couldn't see me or that the powder was just too much for them to take. I knew I had to act fast, so I put another big shot of dust in the air and then jammed the duster rod through the cloth of the couch and plunged that duster as hard as I could 2 or 3 times and then headed for the bannister. I really don't remember how I got down so fast, or how I made it through that job without being stung or hurt. I'm sure the dust was not the greatest thing for me to breathe at the time but without it, I think the alternative would have been much worse. The next day when my service manager tried to reschedule the job, the tenants told him the bees died on their own and they didn't need us anymore. I figured it was best to leave the 'money in the couch' with that one and didn't say a word.

# In The Line Of Fire

Some of you may know I love scenario paintball and I play almost whenever and where ever I can. The only problem with it is, the local field owners know I kill bugs for a living so quite often they'll trade out my services for free games. I call this a problem because of an incident back in the 90's. Sometimes all the free play in the world can't make up for the crazy stunts you have to pull off doing pest control in a battle field.

There I was in the field of action, surrounded in a huge fire fight in the middle of an 80 acre wooded field. With paintballs whizzing by my head, I could hear the game director on the loud speaker frantically calling my name. *"Jerry Schappert-The Bug Doctor, Come To The Office Right Away!"* My first thoughts were that I had an emergency at home but when I got up to the staging area I saw two players that were in enormous pain writhing about and the people around them desperately wiping and brushing something off them. When I got to them, I saw that they were trying to remove literally hundreds of stingers still lodged in their bodies, as well as pulsing venom sacs that looked like something out of a Stephen King movie.

The owner of the field was panicked and wanted me to get out there and do something, anything to kill those bees. I didn't have any equipment with me so I rushed to my house to get my service truck and filled my lawn rig with insecticide. I didn't know where this nest was located exactly and I figured I might not be able to get very close with my truck. I had done bee and yellow jacket nests on paintball fields before but never during a game so I knew I may need all 300 feet of my rigs hose. As it turned out, I did.

I was able to get within about 100 feet with my truck but no closer, so I fired up my engine and started for the nest. What surprised me however, was that my opposition was not only the bees, but the players on the field. You see in paintball we wear masks and certain color tape to identify who's who. Also, the promoters of the game allow tanks (converted vans or golf carts) and all sorts of wild looking weaponry. (If you've never tried it, believe me, you would love it.) So here I with an impressive looking lawn GUN and dragging a long yellow through the woods. Now I was stalking a bee's nest but the enemy players had no idea what I was doing. For all they knew, I had some high powered weapon with a long hose for constant air supply and they let me have it. I was taking paintball shots from every direction but I couldn't shoot back or stop them. At one point I just had to stop and put my head down as a crazy volley of paint pummeled me and I couldn't move ahead until they stopped. Sure I was worried about the huge nest in the ground that I had to deal with but I wasn't sure if getting stung by thousands of bees would hurt any less than the 10,000 hits I just took. Dripping with paint and probably looking pathetic the referees stepped in and the firing stopped.

With some freedom to move about I was able to shoot the nest from a safe distance and finally eradicate the nest. I was never stung a single time but you would have never known it looking at my welts from all the paintballs later that day. Good thing I wasn't allergic to paint, because I was definitely in, the firing line.

Jerry Schappert